Barack Obama
FOR BEGINNERS®
AN ESSENTIAL GUIDE

Barack Obama
FOR BEGINNERS®
AN ESSENTIAL GUIDE

BY BOB NEER • ILLUSTRATED BY JOE LEE

FOR BEGINNERS®

an imprint of Steerforth Press
Hanover, New Hampshire

For Beginners LLC
62 East Starrs Plain Road
Danbury, CT 06810 USA
www.forbeginnersbooks.com

Text: © 2009 Bob Neer
Illustrations: © 2009 Joe Lee
Cover Photo: AP Photo/Jae C. Hong
Cover/Book Design: David Janik

This book was prepared without the involvement of any political party or campaign.

A For Beginners® Documentary Comic Book
Copyright © 2009

Cataloging-in-Publication information is available from the Library of Congress.

ISBN# 978-1-934389-44-7

Manufactured in the United States of America

For Beginners® and Beginners Documentary Comic Books® are published by For Beginners LLC.

Second Edition

10 9 8 7 6 5 4 3 2

06 09

Table of Contents

Complete notes, including one-click links to source materials where available, links to video clips, a timeline, and additional information about For Beginners, can be found at Barack-ObamaforBeginners.com. Visit us online!

I. ORIGINS 1961-1985

Barack Obama, the 44th President of the United States, is a blend of extraordinary diversity: parents from Kenya and Kansas; an education in Indonesia, Hawaii, California, New York, and Massachusetts; employment in Chicago's poorest communities, leading law firms, and premier university; best-selling books that merge personal history and political action; and elected positions in the Illinois and United States Senates before the Presidency.

The result is a politician who asserts that we all are linked, and that while idealism must serve realism, pragmatism requires purpose. His latest book, which carries the inspirational title *The Audacity of Hope*, contains the following conclusion: "We should be guided by what works."

The Obama family traces its modern lineage to Hussein Onyango Obama, a Kenyan member of the Luo tribe born in 1895 near Lake Victoria. Onyango was a restless man of ambition. He was one of the first in his village to wear western clothing, walked for two weeks to Nairobi to find work, braving leopards and other dangers, and served with the British armed forces in World War I. He visited Europe, Myanmar and Sri Lanka as a soldier and briefly converted to Christianity, but abandoned it for Islam and added "Hussein" to his name after the war. He was arrested by British colonial authorities in 1949 during the struggle for Kenyan independence, tortured and jailed for two years, but eventually found innocent and released, after which he returned to his homeland.

Obama's father, Barack Hussein Obama, Sr., was born in 1936 in Nyangoma-Kogelo, Siaya District, also near Lake Victoria, to Onyango's second wife Habiba Akumu. She quarreled with her husband and left when her son was nine. The boy was raised by Onyango's third wife Sarah. He was a precocious student but chafed at traditional village employment, which included tending goats. He took success in high school for granted, became boastful and truculent, and was expelled. He squabbled with his father, left the family lands, married his first wife Kezia in 1954 at age 18, and by his early 20s found himself employed as a shop boy in Nairobi with two children and little money. A pair of American teachers befriended him and helped him apply to U.S. universities. In 1959 he secured admission, after many rejections, to the University of Hawaii to study economics: the institution's first African student. A scholarship program organized by Kenyan politicians and financed by over 8,000 American donors paid for his studies.

Obama, Sr. wore religion lightly. "Although my father had been raised a Muslim, by the time he met my mother he was a confirmed atheist, thinking religion to be so much superstition," his son has written. Indeed Sarah, the step-mother who raised Obama Sr., has said her step-son was never a muslim.

Obama's mother's family history begins with her parents Madelyn Payne and Stanley Dunham—grandparents of Barack

Obama who cared for him during high school. Payne was a Kansan raised in Wichita by "stern Methodist parents who did not believe in drinking, playing cards or dancing." Nonetheless, their daughter, one of the best students in her high school graduating class, often went downtown to listen to big bands. On one of these outings she met Stanley Dunham, originally from the oil-town of El Dorado, Kansas, a furniture salesman "who could charm the legs off a couch." Dunham was a Baptist from the "other side of the railroad tracks." (It later emerged that he was also a seventh cousin, once removed, of Vice-President Dick Cheney and also a seventh cousin, twice removed, of President Harry S. Truman.) Payne's family did not approve of the liaison, and the pair married in secret a few weeks before Madelyn graduated from high school. She told her parents after she received her diploma.

During World War II, Dunham joined the Army and served under General George S. Patton. Madelyn worked on a Boeing B-29 assembly line in Wichita. Obama's mother, Stanley Ann Dunham, was born in 1942 at Fort Leavenworth, Kansas. Her father wanted a boy, thus the name, which grieved the girl.

Dunham moved the family frequently: California, Kansas, Texas, and finally Mercer Island in Washington state—now a high end home for wealthy Seattle residents, then a somewhat isolated and bucolic suburb. Madelyn became vice-president of a local bank. The family attended the East Shore Unitarian Church. Stanley Ann—she dutifully carried the first name through her mid-teens—thrived in the intellectual atmosphere of the local high school, where her philosophy teacher challenged his classes with texts like *The Organization Man*, *The Hidden Persuaders*, and *1984*. The precocious student was offered admission to the University of Chicago in 1958 at the age of 16, but her father said she was too young to go.

In 1960, Ann graduated from high school and the family moved to Hawaii. Stanley got a job at a large furniture store, Madelyn at the Bank of Hawaii, and they bought a house near the University of Hawaii. Ann, 18, enrolled as a freshman. In a Russian language class, she met Barack Obama, Sr., 23, who told her he was divorced. They gathered with friends on weekends to listen to jazz and discuss politics and world affairs. Ann was the only woman. She was "the original feminist," according to Neil Abercrombie, now a Democratic congressman from Hawaii who participated in the meetings.

On 2 February 1961, the pair slipped away to Maui and were married. The wedding—Obama "black as pitch," Ann "white as milk"—would have been illegal in 22 states. Ann dropped out of college. On 4 August Barack Hussein Obama Jr. was born at the Kapi' olani Medical Center in Honolulu.

The couple moved into a small apartment near the university. The following year, just three years after he had arrived, Obama Sr. completed his studies. He obtained two offers of admission to Ph.D. programs in economics. The first, from Harvard, did not include enough funding to support his family. The second, from the New School in New York, included a more generous stipend. Obama chose Harvard, and did not take his family to Cambridge.

In 1963, Ann returned to college. Food stamps helped support the family. After two years, her husband still absent, she filed for divorce.

At the East-West Center at the university she met Lolo Soetoro, an Indonesian student. In 1967, he proposed, she graduated, and the three moved to his home on the outskirts of Jakarta. Soetoro, who was drafted into the Indonesian Army as a lieutenant on his return, was not wealthy—they had no air conditioning, refrigerator, flush toilet, or car—but the six year old Obama was impressed nonetheless. His step-father had acquired a pet monkey for him. Baby crocodiles inhabited the garden. He learned to speak Indonesian and attended the local Catholic Franciscus Assisi Primary School. "The children of farmers, servants and low-level bureaucrats had become my friends, and together we ran the streets morning and night, hustling odd jobs, catching crickets, battling swift kites with razor-sharp lines— the loser watching his kite soar off with the wind," he wrote later in his memoir. His mother was hired to teach english at the U.S. embassy.

The family prospered when Soetoro was discharged and got a job in the government relations office of a U.S. oil firm. They moved to the affluent Menteng neighborhood and acquired a refrigerator, television, and car and driver. Obama transferred to SDN Menteng 1, an elite secular public elementary school that served primarily middle- and upper-class children, including several grandchildren of Indonesian President Suharto. He was the only foreigner.

For administrative purposes, Obama was registered as a Muslim at this school, as at the Catholic institution, because that was the religion of his stepfather. He learned about Islam for two hours each week. His mother did not belong to any denomination. Nonetheless, Obama wrote, "My mother was in many ways the most spiritually awakened person I have ever known. . . . She possessed an abiding sense of wonder, a reverence for life and its precious, transitory nature." As a child, she would wake him to see a spectacular moon, or tell him to close his eyes to listen to the rustle of leaves as they walked together at twilight. "But she had a healthy skepticism of religion as an institution. And as a consequence, so did I." His step-father enjoyed alcohol and was not devout. Obama has never been a practicing Muslim.

The harshness of life was never distant in Jakarta. Later, Obama remembered "The face of the man who had come to our door one day with a gaping hole where his nose should have been: the whistling sound he made as he asked my mother for food. . . . The time that one of my friends told me in the middle of recess that his baby brother had died the night before of an evil spirit brought in by the wind."

His mother understood. "She had learned . . . the chasm that separated the life chances of an American from those of an Indonesian. She knew which side of the divide she wanted her child to be on. I was an American, she decided, and my true life lay elsewhere," Obama wrote.

The means she chose to achieve this end was education. The family did not have enough money for their son to attend a private international school, so his mother subscribed to a series of elementary school correspondence courses. Each weekday, Obama remembered, "She came into my room at four in the morning, force-fed me breakfast, and proceeded to teach me my English lessons for three hours before I left for school and she went to work. I offered stiff resistance to this regimen, but in response to every strategy I concocted, whether unconvincing ('My stomach hurts') or indisputably true (my eyes kept closing every five minutes), she would patiently repeat her most powerful defense: 'This is no picnic for me either, buster.'"

She also taught him values. "'If you want to grow into a human being,' she would say to me, 'you're going to need some values.' Honesty . . . Fairness . . . Straight talk . . . and independent judgment," Obama wrote. "In a land where fatalism remained a necessary tool for enduring hardship, where ultimate truths were kept separate from day-to-day realities, she was a lonely witness for secular humanism, a soldier for New Deal, Peace Corps, position-paper liberalism," he added.

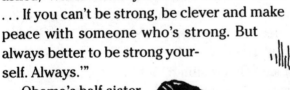

His stepfather taught him how to fight, and about the nature of power. One afternoon he laced boxing gloves onto the boy's hands. "My hands dangled at my sides like bulbs at the ends of thin stalks. . . . He adjusted my elbows, then crouched into a stance and started to bob. 'You want to keep moving, but always stay low—don't give them a target. How does that feel?'" Obama wrote. Later he offered advice. "'The strong man takes the weak man's land. He makes the weak man work in his fields. If the weak man's woman is pretty, the strong man will take her.' He paused to take another sip of water, then asked, 'Which would you rather be?' . . . 'Better to be strong . . . If you can't be strong, be clever and make peace with someone who's strong. But always better to be strong yourself. Always.'"

Obama's half-sister, Maya Soetoro, was born in 1970.

By 1971, the correspondence courses were complete. His grandfather, who had abandoned the furniture business for insurance sales, enlisted the help of his boss, an alumnus, to gain admission for Obama to Punahou Academy, founded in 1841: the most prestigious private school in Hawaii. Current tuition for the school is $15,725 a year. Obama won a scholarship. "My first experience with affirmative action, it seems, had little to do with race," he wrote. He returned to Hawaii in the summer, moved back in with his grandparents, who now lived in a modest two bedroom apartment, and started fifth grade.

The new school was a shock: socially, culturally, and racially. Many of the other fifth graders had been together since kindergarten, Obama's Indonesian sandals were dowdy and his clothes out of style, and he was one of just two black children in the class. Happily, his mother and sister joined him after only a few months: Ann had been admitted to study the anthropology of Indonesia in a master's program at the University of Hawaii.

Just weeks after Ann's return, Obama's father unexpectedly announced that he was coming for a visit. He had received an M.A. from Harvard, taken a job with a U.S. oil company, returned to Kenya, married a woman he met in Cambridge named Ruth Nidesand, and fathered two children with her. He also continued to see his first wife and their children. He worked as an economist for the Kenyan Ministry of Transportation and later as a senior economist in the Kenyan Ministry of Finance, before falling out with Kenya's President Kenyatta. He then lost his position and began a decline into poverty and drinking from which he never recovered. He had been in a car accident and decided to spend a month in Hawaii to recuperate. Obama's time with his father was short, but poignant. "For brief spells in the day I will lie beside him, the two of us alone in the apartment sublet from a retired old woman whose name I forget . . . and I read my book while he reads his. He remains opaque to me . . . But I grow accustomed to his company," he wrote. "Two weeks later he was gone," he added. Forever.

The postscript to the story of Obama's father was a sad one. He was divorced from Ruth and experienced a period of destitution. He suffered another bad automobile accident. Both legs were amputated and he lost his job. He married for a fourth time, despite continued problems with alcohol, and had a son. He died in 1982 at age 46 in a final automobile accident. Obama learned of his death, a few months after his 21st birthday, in a brief telephone call from a relative in Kenya he had never met.

Ann and the children moved into a small apartment and made do on her graduate student grants. Their circumstances were a sharp contrast to the affluence of some of Obama's classmates. "Sometimes, when I brought friends home after school, my mother would hear them remark about the lack of food in the fridge or the less-than-stellar housekeeping, and she would pull me aside and let me know that she was a single mother going to school again and raising two kids, so that baking cookies wasn't exactly at the top of her priority list," he recalled. Lolo visited occasionally from Jakarta.

His mother persevered. She completed her master's degree and advanced to a Ph.D. program in anthropology. In 1975, she finished her coursework and returned to Indonesia with Maya to do field work. Obama, about to begin high school, chose to remain in Hawaii and moved back in with his grandparents.

This was a time of searching. "I was trying to raise myself to be a black man in America, and beyond the given of my appearance, no one around me seemed to know exactly what that meant," Obama wrote. He looked for answers in books, and read the works of great black American intellectuals: James Baldwin, Ralph Ellison, Langston Hughes, Richard Wright, and W. E. B. DuBois. Each of these men, however, wound up disappointed and withdrawn. Only Malcolm X's autobiography, his repeated acts of self-creation, Obama wrote, offered something different. But even that did not provide the answers he needed. He found himself "utterly alone."

He sought a release through drugs: marijuana, alcohol, and sometimes cocaine when he could afford it. "I got high . . . [to] push questions of who I was out of my mind," he remembered.

Over time, he adopted two responses to race-based realities in the culture around him. At the broadest level, he accepted, did not blame, and hoped for change. He told an African American friend who urged him to push for more basketball playing time, for example, that the other players, "play like white boys do, and that's the style coach likes us to play, and they're winning the way they play. I don't play that way." He could see the possibility, however, of a more inclusive society—

he longed for it—and began to consider how he and others might work proactively to bring about change. What he sought to avoid was "withdrawal into a smaller and smaller coil of rage, until being black meant only the knowledge of your own powerlessness, of your own defeat." As a practical matter, he wrote, "People were satisfied so long as you were courteous and didn't make any sudden moves."

An important early decision Obama made was where to go to college. It is possible in retrospect to see his choice of Occidental College in Los Angeles as a first step toward broader opportunities on the mainland. That is not how Obama saw it. He had met a girl from Brentwood, a wealthy neighborhood in the city, on vacation in Hawaii and wanted to be closer to her. So he chose Occidental, which also offered a full scholarship, from among the several schools to which he had been admitted, and enrolled in 1979.

Obama spent his first years in college having a good time. He studied, but not too seriously. He dabbled in politics, including some work on the campus campaign to urge Occidental to divest from South Africa, but not too deeply. He started down the same road of withdrawal and anger he had traveled in Honolulu. Then, after a long night of smoking, drinking, and listening to Billie Holiday, he considered challenges thrown at him by some of his peers at the college, and had an epiphany. "I rose from my couch and opened my front door, the pent-up smoke trailing me out of the room like a spirit. . . . Who told you that being honest was a white thing? they asked me. Who sold you this bill of goods, that your situation exempted you from being thoughtful or diligent or kind, or that morality had a color? You've lost your way, brother. Your ideas about yourself—

about who you are and who you might become—have grown stunted and narrow and small." Years later, Obama had this to say about his early, angry incarnation: "You know, what puzzles me is why people are puzzled by that. That angry character lasts from the time I was fifteen to the time I was twenty-one or so. I guess my explanation is I was an adolescent male with a lot of hormones and an admittedly complicated upbringing. But that wasn't my natural temperament."

A second important decision, to transfer to Columbia College in 1981 through a program arranged between the two schools, was more purposeful. Columbia offered the diversity of a great university; its Harlem neighborhood a large black community; and New York the eclecticism of the country's largest city. Obama wanted all of this.

His introduction to Manhattan, however, was rough: he couldn't get into his apartment on his first night, and had to sleep propped up on his luggage in a vacant lot next door. While he moved on, his mother's second marriage crumbled: she divorced his stepfather in 1980.

As his father had done at a similar age Obama, perhaps aware that the chips were down, now threw himself into his studies. He participated little in campus activities but devoted himself to philosophy and the intricacies of the university's offerings in political science and international relations, including a lengthy honors seminar paper on Soviet nuclear disarmament.

At this point, he decided to try to become a community organizer, to help bring about change in black communities through grassroots efforts. He saw the task as a continuation of the work begun by the civil rights movement: "At night, lying in bed, I would let the slogans drift away, to be replaced with a series of images, romantic images, of a past I had never known. They were of the civil rights movement . . . the same images that my mother had offered me as a child. A pair of college students, hair short, backs straight, placing their orders at a lunch counter teetering on the edge of riot. . . . A county jail bursting with children, their hands clasped together, singing freedom songs." But, he said, he couldn't get an organizing job.

.

Instead, after he received his B.A. from Columbia in 1983, he took a job as a research assistant at Business International, a publishing and advisory firm with about 250 employees worldwide. The company helped U.S. businesses operate overseas. He was soon promoted to the position of financial writer for a reference service called Financing Foreign Operations, and wrote for a newsletter called the *Business International Money Report.* "Forget about this organizing business and do something that's gonna make you some money," advised Ike, the gruff black security guard at his office building.

The pull of his dreams, however, proved too strong. In 1984, Obama resigned. He began to look again for the job he had imagined as a student. He turned down a conference organizing job with a prestigious civil rights organization because, he said, it was too far from the street. He worked for three months at City College in Harlem as an organizer for the New York Public Interest Research Group, an organization founded by Ralph Nader, at a salary of slightly less than $10,000 per year. Obama said he spent the time, "trying to convince minority students at City College about the importance of recycling." Former colleagues say the primary focus of activities was "mass transit, higher education, tuition and financial aid issues." He spent a week handing out leaflets for the campaign of a Brooklyn assemblyman. The candidate lost and the campaign stiffed him on his salary. "In six months I was broke, unemployed, eating soup from a can," Obama remembered

The walls were closing in. He had all but given up. Then, on a visit to the New York Public Library, he browsed through what he later described as a "newsletter for do-gooder jobs." He spotted a help-wanted ad from the Developing Communities Project, a coalition of eight Catholic parishes on the South Side of Chicago, all with black congregations led by white priests. He called. Gerald Kellman, a Jewish convert to Catholicism, called back. He needed an organizer—a black organizer: the South Side is the largest African American community in the country. The salary was $10,000 per year plus a $2,000 travel allowance to buy a car. It would go up if Obama made progress. He was off.

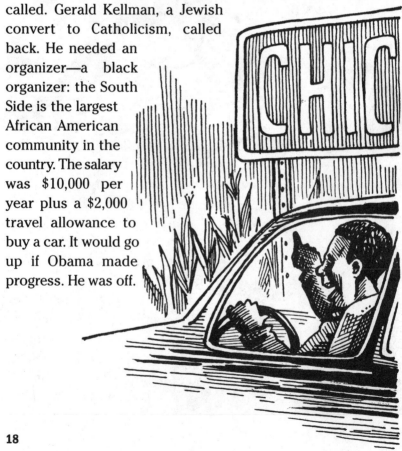

II. ASCENT 1985-96

CAMBRIDGE 1988

CHICAGO 1985

NEW YORK 1983

CHICAGO 1991

Obama arrived in Chicago in June 1985: 23 years old, with a world to conquer. What he found was a physical and spiritual home.

His first assignment was to learn about the South Side. Gerald Kellman sent him to interview residents of Roseland— 97.8 percent African American: a community cut off from the city to the north by two freeways. For the next three weeks, and in a larger sense throughout his years as an organizer, Obama learned the past and present of some of the most disadvantaged people in the country.

His goal was to find issues around which to mobilize: paths to power. In this Kellman and Obama followed precepts laid down by the early Chicago activist Saul Alinsky. "Power comes in two forms—money and people. You haven't got any money, but you do have people," he had advised would-be reformers.

The formula for Obama was less prosaic. "Once I found an issue enough people cared about, I could take them into action. With enough actions, I could start to build power," he wrote.

There was a glimmer here of larger hopes. "The only answer is to build up local power bases that can merge into a national power movement that will ultimately realize your goals," Alinsky averred.

Obama's first major accomplishment, however, came from the top down. He glanced at the back of a brochure from the Mayor's Office of Employment and Training (MET) and noticed the agency had no offices in the southernmost part of the city. He mobilized residents of the Altgeld Gardens housing project—squeezed between a landfill and a redolent sewage treatment plant at the city's southern edge; median household income $11,066 in 2000; also 97 percent African American—and pushed for a jobs center.

City Hall was receptive. Harold Washington, the first African American mayor of Chicago, had been elected in April. Obama organized a public meeting with the director of the MET. He worked his team to exhaustion to ensure a tightly scripted event and a generous turnout. The tenant representatives pushed, and secured a promise for an intake center in six months. "The crowd broke into hearty applause," he remembered. Washington himself opened the office.

His second big effort was more dramatic, but ultimately less satisfying. According to Obama, an Altgeld tenant noticed that the Chicago Housing Authority was soliciting bids for removal of asbestos from the project's Management Office. According to Kellman, Obama himself spotted the bid notice. Either way, the Authority stonewalled tenant demands for an inspection of apartments for asbestos. Obama mobilized a busload of residents and descended on the offices of the executive director. With a few judiciously placed press invitations, the expedition yielded publicity and results. The authority agreed to test every unit. When asbestos was confirmed, stop-gap cleanup measures were instituted. "I changed as a result of that bus trip, in a fundamental way," Obama wrote later.

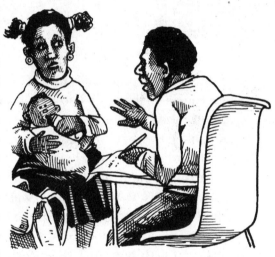

Over the long term, however, little happened to the asbestos in Altgeld. The CHA asked the Department of Housing and Urban Development for over a billion dollars to repair housing projects across the city. The federal agency, which answered to President Reagan, offered money to repair plumbing and roofing problems, or remove asbestos, but not both. The problem remained unresolved during Obama's time as an organizer.

The lesson was plain. Significant change was possible with government support, and impossible without it.

Obama decided that law school would give him tools he needed to do more. Washington, after all, had graduated from the Northwestern University School of Law, and had "parlayed that lofty degree and his own personal charisma into a highly successful political career," in the words of *Chicago Tribune* reporter and Obama biographer David Mendell. "Washington could do more for Chicago's poor blacks with the wave of his veto pen than Obama could in countless days and nights of community meetings in Roseland and Altgeld," Mendell wrote.

He was accepted by Harvard. "I would learn power's currency, in all its intricacy and detail, knowledge that would have compromised me before coming to Chicago but that I could now bring back to where it was needed, back to Roseland, back to Altgeld; bring it back like Promethean fire," the organizer wrote.

On the home front, Obama's existence in Chicago was as austere as in New York. "When I wasn't working, the weekends would usually find me alone in an empty apartment, making do with the company of books," he remembered. A girlfriend who lived with him for a time during this period, and his cat Max, evidently made little impression.

The organizer found spiritual solace, however, at the Trinity United Church of Christ, a South Side megachurch: in the community of its predominantly black congregation of over 10,000, and in the sermons of its minister Jeremiah Wright. Trinity—"Unashamedly Black and Unapologetically Christian" its motto—was the largest church affiliated with the United Church of Christ, a primarily white Protestant Christian denomination with roots in Congregationalism, which branched from Anglo-American Puritanism. Wright, a former marine with degrees from Howard University and the University of Chicago Divinity School, built the church from 87 members in 1972 to over 8,500 by the 1980s. The congregation included people of all races and more than a few celebrities, including television host Oprah Winfrey.

A meeting with Wright, and more generally a "church home," was suggested to Obama as politically expedient by a minister he calls Reverend Philips in his autobiography: "It might help your mission if you had a church home, though. It doesn't matter where, really." He had faith in himself, Obama reflected, but, "Faith in one's self was never enough." He arranged a meeting with Wright.

The Reverend, as Obama described him, was acutely aware of the challenges faced by African Americans. "Life's not safe for a black man in this country, Barack. Never has been. Probably never will be," Obama recalled. The church he built, however, preached inclusion—and there Obama saw power. "By widening its doors to allow all who would enter, a church like Trinity assured its members that their fates remained inseparably bound, that an intelligible 'us' still remained. It was a powerful program, this cultural community, one more pliant than simple nationalism, more sustaining than my own brand of organizing," he concluded.

He woke before dawn on the day of his first visit for services, brushed the lint from his only suit, and arrived by 7:30 a.m. The title of the sermon was, "The Audacity to Hope," a phrase Obama later adapted for the title of his second book *The Audacity of Hope*. "White folks' greed runs a world in need, apartheid in one hemisphere, apathy in another hemisphere . . . That's the world!" Wright preached. But hope, the minister said, could cure those ills, bring us together, and light the way to a future of empathy, inclusiveness, and common purpose. "The audacity of hope! I still remember my grandmother, singing in the house, 'There's a bright side somewhere . . . don't rest until you find it,'" he said.

Obama let his imagination run, and his spirit soared. "At the foot of that cross, inside the thousands of churches across the city, I imagined the stories of ordinary black people merging with the stories of David and Goliath," he wrote later. "The blood that had spilled was our blood, the tears our tears; until this black church, on this bright day, seemed once more a vessel carrying the story of a people into future generations and into a larger world." A child sitting next to him offered him a tissue. He felt tears running down his cheeks, and thanked the boy. Later, despite some continued uncertainty, Obama wrote that he, "submitted myself to His will, and dedicated myself to discovering His truth," and joined the church.

The organizer began at Harvard Law School in the autumn of 1988. As at Columbia, he devoted himself to his studies. He excelled, was elected to the Law Review as one of the approximately 40 top students in his class of about 550, and earned a golden ticket: a lavishly paid job as a summer associate at Sidley & Austin in Chicago.

The 120 year old firm was one of the largest in the country. It was a sign of Obama's appeal that he secured the job after his first year: summer positions, in effect months-long recruiting presentations, were normally reserved for second-year students closer to graduation. Sidley was located in an office tower at the heart of downtown: a metaphor for its place at the center of a network of personal contacts as broad as global business and as local as City Hall. He was in the entry hall of the establishment.

The most lasting connection Obama made at Sidley, however, was to his mentor: a young lawyer named Michelle Robinson, assigned to introduce him to the business. Robinson, one of just 14 African American attorneys among hundreds of lawyers at the firm, was from the South Side. Her father was a city water plant employee, her mother a secretary. Michelle had graduated *cum laude* from Princeton in 1985 with a degree in Sociology, and from Harvard Law in 1988.

More important for Obama, she was charming and attractive. He asked her out. She demurred. He persisted. Finally, she agreed to attend a community-organizing session in a church basement. He delivered a passionate speech, she later recalled, about "the world as it is, and the world as it should be," in his words. On their first big date that summer they went to the Chicago Art Institute, strolled down Michigan Avenue and watched Spike Lee's *Do the Right Thing,* a gripping film about racial and ethnic conflict.

On 5 February 1990, Obama was elected the first African American President of the Law Review. The journal was split between liberal and conservative factions. Obama positioned himself as a centrist, survived a series of run-off elections that reduced the initial field of 18 candidates, and won when the last conservative was

25

voted out and that group swung its support to him. The event was national news and gained him, at 28, a contract for his memoirs. He graduated in 1991.

Obama forsook the corporate world and judicial clerkships that are common destinations for Harvard Law Review presidents, and plunged back into Chicago organizing after law school. His first job was to direct Project Vote!, a registration program inspired by the massive effort that helped elect Washington mayor in 1983. The group had a staff of 10 and attracted 700 volunteers. Driven by its slogan, "It's a Power Thing," the project added more than 150,000 primarily African American voters, of a possible pool estimated at 400,000, to the rolls. For the first time in the city's history registrations in the 19 predominantly black wards outnumbered those in the 19 predominantly white wards. The message, according to Obama: "If the politicians in place now at city and state levels respond to African American voters' needs, we'll gladly work with and support them. If they don't, we'll work to replace them."

Meanwhile, Michelle had left the law firm and, perhaps influenced by her boyfriend, become an assistant to Mayor Daley. She was, she later said, ready to get serious with Obama. He responded with philosophical musings about the value of the institution of marriage. An exchange on these lines sparked a diatribe from her at the end of an elegant restaurant dinner one night in 1991. Dessert arrived, with a box on the plate. Inside, a ring. "He said, 'That kind of shuts you up, doesn't it?'" she recounted later. The couple were married by Wright the following October.

In September 1992, Obama joined the faculty of the University of Chicago Law School as a Lecturer, an adjunct position not eligible for tenure. He taught the basics of constitutional jurisprudence—the history, mechanics and implementation of the Constitution—to a seminar of 20-30 students. A world away, Obama's mother at last completed her almost 1,000 page Ph.D. dissertation on peasant blacksmithing in Indonesia and received her degree. She continued a career she had developed as a global authority on micro-finance lending in developing countries.

In February 1993, Obama added a position at the 12-attorney activist law firm of Davis, Miner, Barnhill & Galland to his list of jobs. He spent most of his time representing community organizers, and pursuing discrimination claims and voting rights cases. The balance of his time was spent preparing legal briefs, contracts and other documents. Notable case work included a lawsuit by the Association of Community Organizations for Reform Now (ACORN) to force the state to implement its Motor Voter Act, and a suit that forced Chicago to redraw some ward boundaries. Perhaps most important, partner Judson Miner, who was Corporation Counsel in Washington's administration until the Mayor died of a sudden heart attack, introduced Obama to his circle of political acquaintances.

The Obamas rose steadily in the Chicago establishment. In 1992, he became a founding

board member of Public Allies, a non-profit that sought to place young leaders in community organizing positions. In 1993, he joined the nine-member board of the Woods Fund, an early supporter of his Developing Communities Project. The next year, he joined the Joyce Foundation's board, another Chicago philanthropy. Michelle became Executive Director of the Chicago office of Public Allies in 1993, after her husband resigned from the board. Throughout this period, during his spare time—generally hours most people sleep, especially those with two jobs—Obama wrote his memoir, *Dreams from My Father: A Story of Race and Inheritance*, which was published in 1995.

In August 1995, the congressman for Illinois' 2nd district was convicted of sexual assault. He resigned, and a special election was called for November. Alice Palmer, the state senator who represented Obama's district, decided to run. She knew her constituent, and his interest in politics, from his organizing and community activity, work on Project Vote!, and association with Davis, Miner. She told Obama she would support him if he wanted to run for her seat. He asked for a commitment that she would not seek re-election to the state Senate even if she lost her bid for Congress. She agreed. Obama, at age 33, launched his first campaign for public office. At the formal kick-off, Palmer had kind words for her chosen successor. "In this room, Harold Washington announced for mayor," she said. "Barack Obama carries on the tradition of independence in this district. . . . His candidacy is a passing of the torch."

Obama's mother was diagnosed with ovarian and uterine cancer the same year. She died in Hawaii on 7 November, aged 52. Her son, immersed in his campaign, was thousands of miles away. He terms this absence the greatest mistake of his life. Stricken, he traveled to Hawaii to help scatter her ashes in the Pacific. "She was the kindest, most generous spirit I have ever known," he wrote in the preface to the 2004 edition of his memoir: "What is best in me I owe to her."

The honeymoon between Palmer and Obama was short. She lost the 1995 special election, changed her mind, and decided to seek re-election to her Illinois Senate seat in the March 1996 Democratic state primary. Her supporters asked Obama to withdraw. He refused. Working quickly, Palmer gathered 1,580 nominating signatures, more than twice the required 757, and filed for the primary just before the December deadline.

Obama called for unity, pragmatism, and a new approach to politics in his campaign. "Any solution to our unemployment catastrophe must arise from us working creatively within a multicultural, interdependent, and international economy," he told the *Chicago Reader* newspaper. "What if a politician were to see his job as that of an organizer, as part teacher and part advocate, one who does not sell voters short but who educates them about the real choices before them?" he mused.

What he practiced, however, was more traditional politics. On the first working day of 1996 Obama's campaign staff, including crack Chicago election law attorney Thomas Johnson, hired specially for the job, started a series of hearings at the Chicago Board of Election Commissioners to challenge the validity of Palmer's signatures, and those of his three other rivals. To those who complained that a voter registration activist and civil rights attorney should not use administrative procedures to limit ballot access, Obama replied that the issue was one of competence: "My conclusion was that if you couldn't run a successful petition drive, then that raised questions in terms of how effective a representative you were going to be." All of his opponents were disqualified, and Obama ran unopposed in the March primary. He cruised to victory in the overwhelmingly Democratic district in the general election, and took his seat in the 59-member Senate in 1997 for a two-year term.

Democrats were in the minority in the Senate, which limited Obama's ability to advance legislation. His supporters did what they could to help. U.S. Senator Paul Simon and Abner Mikva, a former state legislator, Congressional representative from Obama's district, and one-time federal judge, recommended him to Emil Jones, the leader of the Senate Democrats. Jones, a former city sewer inspector from the far South Side, came to view Obama as a son. Obama has called him his "political godfather."

Obama's greatest triumph in his first term was a new ethics and campaign finance bill that prohibited lawmakers from soliciting campaign funds on state property, or accepting gifts from parties with interests in pending legislation. Jones let his friend manage the bill, which passed 52-4 in May 1998. In all, Obama introduced or was chief co-sponsor on 56 bills in his first two years, of which 14 became law. His successes included legislation that increased penalties for criminals who used so-called date rape drugs, improved efficiencies for municipal adjudication procedures, tightened sanctions on felons involved in gun running, and provided compensation to crime victims for some property losses.

On 4 July, Obama became a father when Michelle delivered Malia Ann. That autumn, he was promoted to Senior Lecturer at the University of Chicago Law School. He was responsible for three courses per year, and "regarded as a professor," in the words of the school. In November, he was overwhelmingly re-elected to the Senate for a four-year term.

The first year of his second term was his most successful yet. Obama co-sponsored almost 60 bills, of which 11 became law, almost one each month. The measures focused on health care and child welfare: three examples are increased funding for after-school programs, tightened scrutiny of nursing homes, and improved training in the use of heart defibrillators. With Democrats in the minority, Obama's bills required Republican support for passage; many garnered substantial bipartisan majorities.

Obama, however, was ambitious and sought higher office. He may at one time have aspired to follow Harold Washington as mayor. By 1999, however, Richard M. Daley, the son of longtime Mayor Richard J. Daley, had held that office for a decade. He was as secure in his position as the pope, and proved it in the February election by trouncing his challenger Congressman Bobby Rush, who represented Obama's district.

The Rush campaign had been an incompetent botch. The candidate's car was towed in the middle of a news conference to criticize the city's snow-removal efforts; when the press discovered he had $750 in unpaid parking tickets, he blamed his wife. Obama thought the former alderman, co-founder of the Illinois chapter of the Black Panther Party in 1968, and an incumbent since 1993, was vulnerable. He suspended his law practice and announced his candidacy for Congress in September 1999.

BOBBY
RUSH

Obama's effort suffered setbacks from the start. In October, Rush's son was shot, lingered for four days, and then died. The death prompted a wave of sympathy and forced Obama to stop campaigning for a time. He was attacked as inauthentic—a powerful charge in the heavily African American district. "Barack is viewed in part to be the white man in blackface in our community," said state Senator Donne Trotter, another candidate in the race. In December, in the week between Christmas and New Year's, the Senate unexpectedly scheduled a vote on a closely contested and important piece of gun control legislation. Obama, a supporter of the bill, was on an annual family trip to see his grandmother in Hawaii. His daughter became sick and could not travel. He missed the vote, which failed by three. "Sen. Barack Obama (D-Chicago), who has—had?—aspirations to be a member of Congress, chose a trip to Hawaii over public safety in Illinois," editorialized the *Chicago Tribune.*

The candidate campaigned frenetically. "We called him the Kenyan Kennedy," said a field worker, because he appeared on elevated subway platforms in the dead of winter without an overcoat, hat or gloves. He ultimately won the endorsement of the *Tribune*, but it was not enough. He lost approximately two to one in the March 2000 primary.

Obama's political capital was at a low ebb. So were his personal fortunes: his bank account was empty. The 2000 Democratic Convention was in Los Angeles. He managed a cheap air ticket. When he tried to rent a car, however, his card was rejected. When he finally made it to the convention hall, he wasn't able to get a floor pass. He left disheartened. Then came the 9/11 attacks. After that, "The notion that somebody named Barack Obama could win anything—it just seemed pretty thin," he later remembered. The birth of his second daughter Natasha, nicknamed Sasha, on 7 June must have provided solace.

Hope returned, however, by the summer of 2002. On 5 September 2001 the Illinois Secretary of State pulled the name of a Democrat from a replica of Abraham Lincoln's stovepipe hat, and the party won control of state-wide redistricting that followed the 2000 census. Obama's district was redrawn to include the commercial heart of Chicago: a better base for a bid for higher office. He rejected a run for Attorney General or another state office, and decided to aim for the U.S. Senate. The incumbent, Republican Peter Fitzgerald, was going to retire: the field was open.

PENNY PRITZKER

Big races require big money. A friend lined up a meeting with Penny Pritzker, one of the leaders of a Chicago family with a fortune estimated at around $20 billion, including control of Hyatt Hotels. Late in the summer Obama loaded his wife and their daughters into their car and drove 45 minutes to Pritzker's lakefront summer home. They met. Pritzker approved. Doors to the establishment began to open.

With Pritzker on his side, Obama had the possibility—although not yet the reality—of money. His next step was to hire a consultant to craft his message and manage press coverage and advertising. David Axelrod, a transplanted New Yorker, graduate of the University of Chicago, former *Tribune* reporter, and Communications Director for Paul Simon's 1984 U.S. Senate campaign, won the job for his business AKP Message & Media. He was impressed by Obama, and accepted an unusually small retainer.

Then Obama took a bold step. On 2 October, before a few hundred demonstrators gathered at Federal Plaza in downtown Chicago, he spoke out unequivocally against the invasion of Iraq. "I don't oppose all wars," Obama said, "What I am opposed to is a dumb war. What I am opposed to is a rash war. . . . What I am opposed to is the attempt by political hacks like Karl Rove to distract us from a rise in the uninsured, a rise in the poverty rate, a drop in the median income." It was a hard speech to give, he said later to reporter Mendell: "I was about to announce for the United States Senate and the politics were hard to read then. Bush is at sixty-five percent [approval]. You didn't know whether this thing was gonna play out like the first Gulf War, and you know, suddenly everybody's coming back to cheering." Perhaps as a result, he said, "That's the speech I am most proud of."

DAVID AXELROD

In November Illinois Democrats, after a decade in the minority, regained control of the state Senate. Emil Jones became President. "You know, you have a lot of power," Obama later recalled he told Jones: "You can make the next U.S. senator." Jones, he said, replied, "Wow, that sounds good! Got anybody in mind?" Obama answered: "Yes—me." Jones did just that. He appointed Obama Chair of the Health and Human Services Committee and sent important bills his way. By the end of 2004, Obama had sponsored over 800 pieces of legislation. His accomplishments, in addition to his ethics reforms, included a bill that required police to audio- or videotape homicide interrogations, which was passed unanimously by the Senate; leadership of legislation to outlaw racial profiling; and death penalty reform.

In January 2004, with a framework for his fundraising and political operations in place, and a solid legislative track record, Obama announced his candidacy for the U.S. Senate.

The state legislator polled third behind two main opponents among eight declared Democratic candidates. Blair Hull was a professional blackjack player who invested his winnings in a securities trading business he later sold for $531 million. He was believed to be the richest person ever to seek office in Illinois. Dan Hynes, the state comptroller, came from a politically connected family. His father Thomas had been the Cook County assessor—a powerful position in Chicago—and President of the Illinois Senate.

Hull announced he would spend $40 million to win the race. He hired a large team of top consultants, acquired a giant campaign bus, and plastered the state with advertisements. In short order, he was the front-runner.

But he had an Achilles heel. He had been married and divorced twice from his second wife. The papers of the second separation were sealed. Local media outlets sued to have them released on the grounds that Hull's candidacy warranted an exceptional level of public scrutiny. When it appeared likely, a few weeks before the election, that a judge would agree, Hull and his former wife Brenda Sexton released the records themselves. They were explosive. On one instance, Sexton claimed, Hull "hung on the canopy bar of my bed, leered

at me and stated, 'Do you want to die? I am going to kill you . . .'"
He had been arrested for allegedly hitting her, although authorities declined to press charges. Hull persevered in the race, but his support evaporated.

Obama then made short work of Hynes. His campaign theme, "Yes, we can," devised by Axelrod, caught the imagination of the electorate. His television advertisements galvanized support in the African American community, and ultimately yielded 95 percent of their votes. In March 2004, he won the Democratic primary with 53 percent of the ballots compared to 24 percent for Hynes and about 10 percent for Hull.

Success had its price. Obama seemed diffident as victory appeared to draw close. Supporter Valerie Jarrett asked why he seemed down. "When he lifted his head to answer, a tear rolled down his cheek. 'I'm really going to miss those little girls,' he said," she recalled.

The Republican nominee in the general election was Jack Ryan, a handsome former investment banker worth as much as $96 million who also was willing to spend huge sums to win. Obama had the help of the well heeled, like George Soros, and the well connected, like Hillary Clinton, but he could not raise an unlimited amount.

Remarkably, Ryan suffered much the same fate as Hull. He too had sealed divorce papers. He too faced a lawsuit from media outlets. When the files finally were opened in June they showed he had taken his wife Jeri, an actress who appeared on the television program Star Trek, among other roles, to sex clubs in New York and Paris, and tried to force her to have sex with him in front of strangers. Ryan withdrew from the race three days later, leaving Obama without a Republican opponent.

A new star twinkled in the political firmament of the Democratic Party. Soon, Obama would shine even brighter. John Kerry, the Democratic nominee for president, asked him, still just a state senator, to deliver the keynote address at the Democratic National Convention in Boston. The slot carried live nationwide prime time television coverage and the attention of the world's media.

Obama titled the speech, "The Audacity of Hope," inspired by Reverend Wright's sermon. He began with his own story. "Let's face it, my presence on this stage is pretty unlikely," he said. He applauded American exceptionalism: "In no other country on Earth is my story even possible," he continued. We share common values, he asserted. "This year, in this election, we are called to reaffirm our values and our commitments, to hold them against a hard reality and see how we are measuring up, to the legacy of our forbearers and the promise of future generations." The country, he maintained, had not met that measure. "And fellow Americans, Democrats, Republicans, independents, I say to you, tonight, we have more work to do . . ."

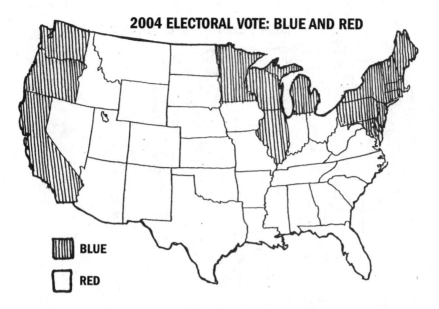

2004 ELECTORAL VOTE: BLUE AND RED

▥ BLUE

☐ RED

The only way to solve our problems, Obama argued, is together: "It is that fundamental belief—I am my brother's keeper, I am my sister's keeper—that makes this country work." He expanded on that idea in the heart of his address: "Now even as we speak, there are those who are preparing to divide us, the spin masters and negative ad peddlers who embrace the politics of anything goes. Well, I say to them tonight, there's not a liberal America and a conservative America; there's the United States of America. There's not a black America and white America and Latino America and Asian America; there's the United States of America. The pundits, the pundits like to slice and dice our country into red states and blue States: red states for Republicans, blue States for Democrats. But I've got news for them, too. We worship an awesome God in the blue states, and we don't like federal agents poking around our libraries in the red states. We coach little league in the blue states and, yes, we've got some gay friends in the red states. There are patriots who opposed the war in Iraq, and there are patriots who supported the war in Iraq. We are one people, all of us pledging allegiance to the stars and stripes, all of us defending the United States of America."

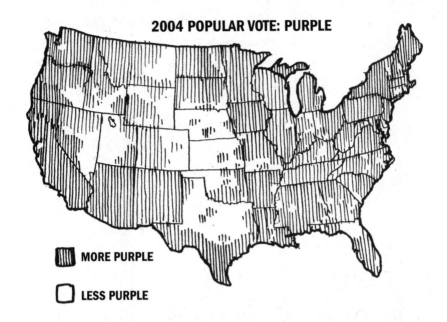

2004 POPULAR VOTE: PURPLE

▦ **MORE PURPLE**

▢ **LESS PURPLE**

Finally, he concluded, we must have hope: "Hope in the face of difficulty, hope in the face of uncertainty, the audacity of hope: In the end, that is God's greatest gift to us, the bedrock of this nation, a belief in things not seen, a belief that there are better days ahead." Reaction was overwhelmingly positive. Obama became famous.

ALAN KEYES

The beleaguered Illinois Republican Party threw Maryland resident and two-time losing G.O.P. presidential candidate Alan Keyes into the race in August. The former U.S. ambassador to the U.N. Economic and Social Conference under President Reagan had never lived in Illinois and never won an election. Obama beat him 70 percent to 29 percent, the largest margin of victory ever in an Illinois Senate election. He resigned from the state Senate and

40

the University of Chicago and was sworn in to the U.S. Senate, the fifth African American ever elected to that house, by his distant relative Vice President Dick Cheney on 4 January 2005.

The wind was at Obama's back. In October 2006 his second book, *The Audacity of Hope*, written in his spare time during his first year in the Senate, was released. It rose to the top of the *New York Times* bestseller list. Works by potential 2008 Democratic presidential candidates Hillary Clinton and John

Edwards languished far down on the list. Enormous enthusiastic crowds gathered for book signings at venues across the country. They attracted reporters who filed stories that further built attention. His advisors urged him to run for president. "He's ready, why wait? Obama in '08" read a popular Washington D.C. bumper sticker. "The iron can't get any hotter," he told a friend.

He consulted with Michelle. She said if he stopped smoking—a habit he had struggled with for years—she would support a bid. He quit.

On 11 February 2007, Obama stood in front of a crowd of 15,000 at the Illinois state capital, and announced his candidacy for president. "In the face of war, you believe there can be peace. In the face of despair, you believe there can be hope. In the face of a politics that's shut you out, that's told you to settle, that's divided us for too long, you believe we can be one people, reaching for what's possible, building that more perfect union," he said. "Each and every time, a new generation has risen up and done what's needed to be done. Today we are called once more—and it is time for our generation to answer that call. Together, starting today, let us finish the work that needs to be done, and usher in a new birth of freedom on this Earth," he continued. The race was on.

IV. PRIMARY CAMPAIGN, FEBRUARY 2007-JUNE 2008

Obama built his run for president on relatively centrist positions, opposition to the war in Iraq, and a campaign operation that integrated community organizing techniques with the power of the Internet. He attended to both policy and practice on the day he announced his candidacy: first, he released a 63-page "Blueprint for Change," which described his platform; second, he launched a set of organizing tools at My.BarackObama.com. The result was a campaign whose message was delivered from the top down, but whose activism grew from the bottom up. Fundraising was everyone's job. Key elements of his successful U.S. Senate drive—the themes of unity and change, "Yes We Can" slogan (now capitalized and without punctuation), and top operatives—formed the core of his national effort.

Pragmatism was his policy touchstone. "We will do collectively, through our government, only those things that we cannot do as well or at all individually and privately," he wrote, quoting Lincoln.

Opportunity was the focus of his economic plan. Upward mobility, "has been at the heart of this country's promise since its founding," he wrote. "The resources and power of the national government can facilitate, rather than supplant, a vibrant free market," he added. He called for a middle class tax cut of up to $500 per person, or $1,000 per working family; repeal of the Bush administration's tax breaks for households that earn over $250,000; an increased minimum wage indexed to inflation; tighter regulation of the consumer credit industry to facilitate product comparisons, ensure that risks in credit card and mortgage offers were explained, and outlaw usurious practices; trade agreements that "spread good labor and environmental standards," including a "fix" for NAFTA; and expansion of the threshold for Family and Medical Leave Act coverage from firms with over 50 employees to those with more than 25 employees.

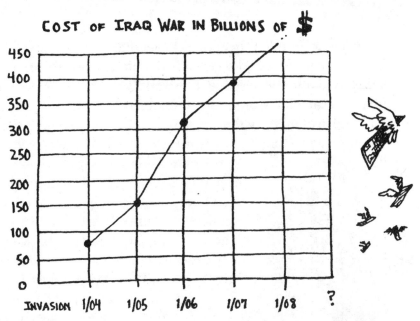

COST OF IRAQ WAR IN BILLIONS OF $

450
400
350
300
250
200
150
100
50
0

INVASION 1/04 1/05 1/06 1/07 1/08 ?

He was unequivocal about Iraq: the war "should never have been authorized and should never have been waged." The U.S. should withdraw all combat brigades within 16 months, he wrote, and should not maintain permanent bases. A residual force could protect diplomats and, if necessary, carry out strikes against al Qaeda. In Afghanistan, however, he argued the U.S. should "finish the fight" and crack down on "al Qaeda safe havens in Pakistan."

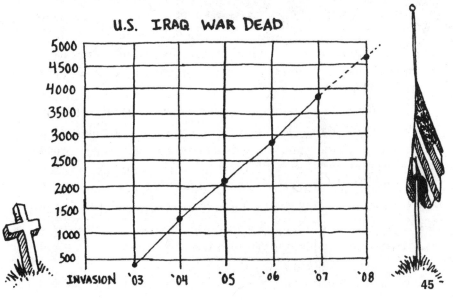

U.S. IRAQ WAR DEAD

5000
4500
4000
3500
3000
2500
2000
1500
1000
500

INVASION '03 '04 '05 '06 '07 '08

With respect to foreign policy in general, he urged less unilateralism and more diplomacy: the U.S. should talk "to our foes as well as our friends." He said he would meet the President of Iran, for example, without preconditions—but refused to rule out the use of military force against the Islamic Republic. The Guantanamo Bay military prison, he said, should be closed.

He framed energy policy as a matter of national security: "A nation that can't control its energy sources can't control its future." He urged $15 billion in annual investments for a decade in biofuels and fuel infrastructure, hybrids, low emission coal plants, and a more efficient digital electricity grid. Research on clean energy projects including biomass, solar and wind energy, he said, should be doubled, and a requirement imposed that 25 percent of electricity be generated from clean, sustainable sources by 2025. He proposed a mandatory cap-and-trade system to create a market for carbon emissions, and reduce them 80 percent below 1990 levels by 2050.

"In a world where knowledge determines value in the job market ... too many of America's schools are not holding up their end of the bargain," he wrote of education. "American 15 year olds rank 28th out of 40 countries in mathematics and 19th out of 40 countries in science," he added. The U.S. "has one of the highest dropout rates in the industrialized world." He suggested Early Learning Challenge Grants to help states move toward voluntary, universal pre-school; an expanded national program of affordable high-quality child care; proper funding of the No Child Left Behind program; Teacher Service Scholarships to cover four years of undergraduate or two years of graduate teacher education; and an American Opportunity Tax Credit to fund the first $4,000 of annual college expenses—two-thirds of tuition at an average public tertiary institution and enough to pay for all of community college for most students.

Finally, he urged that a new national affordable health care plan, similar to the one provided to members of Congress, be offered to all citizens regardless of employer. Subsidies would allow the less affluent to purchase the new plan or private alternatives. Coverage would be required for all children. Efficiency, he said, could be increased through stronger insurance industry antitrust laws; improved disclosure regulations; permission for patients to purchase drugs made in "developed countries if the drugs are safe;" and an annual investment of $10 billion dollars for five years in medical information technology.

Spring polls showed three leaders in the race for the Democratic nomination: New York Senator and former First Lady Hillary Clinton with about 35 percent of voters, Obama with around 25 percent, and former North Carolina Senator and 2004 vice presidential candidate John Edwards with 10-15 percent. The other candidates, New Mexico Governor Bill Richardson, Connecticut Senator Chris Dodd, Delaware Senator Joe Biden, Ohio Congressman Dennis Kucinich, and former Alaska Senator Mike Gravel, lagged far behind.

Behind the scenes, Obama's staff used the Internet to build a nationwide volunteer organization, and fundraising juggernaut. The campaign website allowed individuals to stay informed about national and local efforts; make telephone calls to voters through a central database and update records based on results; and start mini-campaigns, complete with fundraising systems, blogs and events, to organize people in their geographic area or with shared interests. Managers guided the torrent of activism harnessed by the system first to one battleground, then another.

The public responded. On 16 January, a University of North Dakota graduate started "Barack Obama (One Million Strong for Barack)," on the Facebook social networking site. The group attracted over 100,000 members in nine days: one of the fastest growth rates ever seen at Facebook. There were more than 250,000 members when Obama officially launched his campaign on 11 February. The biggest pro-Clinton group on the site at the time had just 3,251 members. Chris Hughes, Facebook's co-founder, joined Obama's campaign that month. An "Obama application" on Facebook, that tied together these hundreds of thousands of supporters, soon appeared.

The impact of these grassroots efforts became clear on 31 March when fundraising reports for the first quarter—the so-called "first primary"—were released. Obama was much closer to Clinton than the polls suggested. The New York Senator had collected $26 million, Obama $25.6 million, and Edwards $12 million. The other candidates were literally out of the money. Crucially, although their gross totals were similar, the average size of Obama's donations was much smaller than those for Clinton. Obama, unlike Clinton, also refused to accept money from lobbyists. In sum, the Illinois Senator had a broader base of financial support.

Obama maintained his grip on the imagination of Internet users and younger voters throughout the summer and fall as the candidates criss-crossed the country to gain media attention, meet voters, and raise money. His youth, campaign themes, relative centrism, and opposition to the Iraq war were key selling points. In June, a YouTube video called "I Got a Crush on Obama" featuring a scantily dressed "Obama Girl" who crooned her affection for the candidate and dismissed his rivals, became a hit. Several million people watched it. On 2 July, the campaign announced Obama had raised $32 million in the second quarter, far above the previous record for the period and more than Clinton's $27 million and Edwards' $9 million. Obama had 154,000 contributors, more than double the 60,000 who donated to Clinton. In December, there was a wave of publicity when billionaire Oprah Winfrey, host of the most popular television talk show in the country, endorsed him.

The Iowa caucuses, held on 3 January 2008, were the first vote of the campaign. Party members assembled in 1,784 locations, one for each precinct, across the state. Arcane procedures governed the assemblies. Clinton was expected to do well because of her deep connections to party leaders—the result of eight years as first lady and seven as a senator. Some observers harbored concerns that an African American candidate would have difficulty in a state that was 94.6 percent white. In the event, turnout shattered expectations: over 227,000 Democrats voted, compared to 122,193 in 2004. Obama's punctilious organization, managed from an overwhelming 37 field offices (none of the other candidates had a comparable ground organization) brought victory. The Illinois Senator won 38 percent of ballots, Edwards 30 percent, and Clinton 29 percent. The message was dramatic: Clinton's nomination was not a forgone conclusion. Obama was a contender.

Destiny was at hand, Obama said in his victory speech. "On this January night—at this defining moment in history—you have done what the cynics said we couldn't do. We are choosing hope over fear. We're choosing unity over division, and sending a powerful message that change is coming to America." He continued, "This was the moment when the improbable beat what Washington always said was inevitable. This was the moment when we tore down barriers that have divided us for too long—when we rallied people of all parties and ages to a common cause; when we finally gave Americans who'd never participated in politics a reason to stand up and to do so. This was the moment when we finally beat back the politics of fear, and doubt, and cynicism; the politics where we tear each other down instead of lifting this country up. This was the moment. Years from now, you'll look back and you'll say that this was the moment—this was the place—where America remembered what it means to hope."

The vote had an immediate impact. Senators Biden and Dodd withdrew from the race. Obama leapt to a 10-point lead in polls for the New Hampshire primary—an election, rather than a series of caucus meetings as in Iowa—scheduled for five days later.

A quartet of bleary candidates—Clinton, Edwards, Obama, and Richardson, the top four finishers in Iowa—gathered 48 hours later in Manchester, New Hampshire, for an ABC News/Facebook debate. Edwards sided with Obama, and attacked Clinton as a standard-bearer for the status quo. "Every time he speaks out for change, every time I fight for change, the forces of the status quo are going to attack—every single time," he said, referencing Obama by his side. The New York senator, playing to her theme of experience, appeared to accept his premise: "We don't need to be raising the false hopes of our country about what can be delivered," she said.

A few days later, Clinton choked up in response to a woman who asked how she persevered despite the strain of the campaign . . . and who did her hair. It was not clear what caused the

spark of
emotion:
the ardu-
ousness of the
campaign, the
reference to her
appearance, which
had little to do with
qualification to be president, or some other reason.
Regardless, the exchange created a surge of publicity for the senator. She defied expectations and narrowly
won the primary with 39 percent of the
vote to 36 percent for Obama, 17 percent
for Edwards, and about five percent for
Richardson. Axelrod delivered the results to
his candidate. "It doesn't look like it's going
to happen," he said. "This is going to take a
while, isn't it?" Obama replied. Richardson, the
first Hispanic candidate for President, withdrew
from the race on 10 January.

Clinton won in Michigan on 15 January with
55 percent of the vote, but the decision was
largely ignored because the state had broken
party rules by scheduling its vote so early
in the process. It consequently was un-
clear whether its delegates would be
seated at the convention. Obama's
name was not on the ballot.

The next two contests were a caucus in Nevada and a primary in South
Carolina. Clinton won the first, 51 percent to 45 percent, but Obama ran
strongly across the state and ultimately
won 13 delegates to her 12. Edwards, who had

taken an increasingly uncompromising anti-business line in his speeches, gained less than five percent of the votes and won no delegates. Kucinich, who had attracted only a tiny fraction of the electorate and had been largely ignored by the media, withdrew from the contest on 24 January.

South Carolina, "Where the Confederate flag still flies," as Obama later said, was the first southern state and the first with a large African American population to hold a primary: just under one-third of its citizens are black. Obama carried it by 55 percent to Clinton's 27 percent—58 percent to her 23 percent among every age group except voters over 65. The race revealed what appeared to be organizational limits in Clinton's campaign, which had focused its resources on earlier states. "Obama's people had been organizing and cleaning lists since August, building an organization with real leadership and a genuine organizing base. . . . The Clinton campaign did not have anything close to that, having spent its time organizing in Iowa, New Hampshire and Nevada," wrote blogger Matt Stoller. When President Clinton compared Obama's win to that of earlier African American presidential candidate Jesse Jackson— "Jesse Jackson won South Carolina in '84 and '88. Jackson ran a good campaign. And Obama ran a good campaign here," he said—blogs erupted in outrage at a perceived racially-charged slight to Obama's achievement.

Obama won significant endorsements after his South Carolina victory. Massachusetts Senator Ted Kennedy, his niece Caroline, daughter of President John F. Kennedy, and his son Patrick, a Rhode Island congressman, endorsed the man whose staff eight years earlier had referred to him as the "Kenyan Kennedy" on 28 January. "I feel change in the air," Senator Kennedy said. Obama "offers that same sense of hope and inspiration" that her father did, Caroline said. On 1 February, the 3.2 million member online activist group MoveOn.org endorsed him, the first Democratic presidential primary endorsement in the organization's history. The group's members, who voted online, favored Obama over Clinton 70 precent to 30 percent.

The New York senator carried Florida 50 percent to 33 percent for Obama at the end of January. As with Michigan, however, the state had broken party rules by scheduling its vote too early; neither candidate campaigned in the state, and it was not clear if its delegates would count toward the nomination. Edwards dropped out on 30 January.

The race was now between Obama and Clinton. There was no clear leader. The fierce contest between two historic rivals riveted domestic and international attention. All eyes turned to 5 February, known as "Super Tues-

day," because on that day voters in 22 states assigned 1,681 delegates. A total of 2,118 delegates was required for nomination. The result was inconclusive: Obama won more states, but Clinton carried the popular vote and gained three more delegates, 837 to 834. News broke the next day that suggested shakiness inside Clinton's campaign: she had been forced to loan her team $5 million at the end of January.

Then Obama began a winning streak that lasted more than a month, encompassed big and small states across the country, and left him with an advantage in delegates, popular perception, and the perception of the approximately 825 unelected "Superdelegate" party insiders, that proved decisive. On 9 February, he won three states and a territory by huge margins: Louisiana 57-36, Nebraska 68-32, Washington 68-31, and the U.S. Virgin Islands 90-8. He won Maine 59-40 on 10 February, the District of Columbia 75-24, Virginia 64-35, and Maryland 61-36 two days later, and Wisconsin 58-41 and Hawaii 76-24 on 19 February. The

victories confirmed what earlier results suggested: Obama's Internet-centered campaign, and his electoral support, had both breadth and depth.

Attention focused on the new frontrunner, and a series of controversies rocked the campaign. On 19 February, Clinton's aides observed that portions of a speech Obama gave three days earlier were similar to an address given in 2006 by his campaign co-chair, Massachusetts Governor Deval Patrick. They suggested plagiarism. Obama dismissed the controversy with ease: he acknowledged Patrick's assistance; the governor said he was flattered; and the public shrugged. A contretemps on 25 February over a 2006 photo of Obama wearing traditional Somali dress—which some tabloids and websites described as "Muslim" clothing—during a visit to Kenya after his election to the U.S. Senate, was equally swiftly dismissed. Senator Dodd, his former rival, endorsed Obama on 26 February.

By 4 March, when Clinton finally won Ohio, Texas and Rhode Island, analysts armed with sharp pencils had concluded that, barring a cataclysm, an Obama nomination was only a matter of time. John McCain clinched the Republican nomination the same evening.

The Clinton campaign waited to see if the trial of Chicago real estate developer Antoin "Tony" Rezko, which began on 6 March, might be cataclysmic for Obama. Rezko was charged with using his clout as an adviser to the Illinois governor to extort money from firms that did business with the state. There was no direct connection between Obama and the charges—but the Presidential candidate had a long history with the defendant. Rezko offered Obama a job when Obama became President of the Harvard Law Review, but the student turned him down. Later, Rezko was a client of his law firm Davis, Miner, and Obama spent five hours on matters related to a partnership between a church group and Rezko's company, the Rezmar corporation, to build low-income housing. In 1997, Allison Davis, a partner at the law firm, left and joined Rezko to form the New Kenwood real estate company. Obama, then a state senator, wrote letters to state and federal officials to urge them to approve a housing development for low-income senior citizens proposed by the company. "It was going to help people in his district," his campaign said in 2007. Finally, Rezko donated numerous times to Obama's campaigns, although not to his presidential bid, and was a member of the finance committee for his U.S. Senate campaign. Total donations from Rezko, his family members, and his associates, to the senate campaign totaled about $250,000.

ANTOIN REZKO

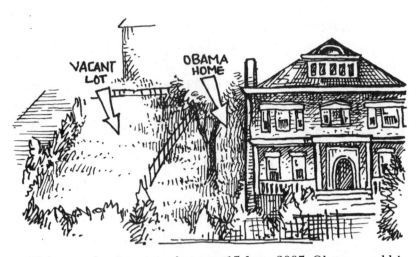

This was the context when, on 15 June 2005, Obama and his wife bought a house for $1.65 million (financed largely by earnings from his writings)—and Rezko's wife bought an adjoining vacant lot on the same day from the same seller for $625,000. The Obamas paid $300,000 below the asking price for the house. Rezko's wife purchased her lot for the asking price. The seller, a doctor, later said the Obamas had made two earlier bids for the house that were even lower, and that the price he accepted was the best he could get. In February 2006, the Obamas bought one-sixth of the lot, a 10-foot strip that ran next to their property, from Rezko's wife for $104,000—one-sixth of the purchase price—to expand their garden. Details of these transactions came to light in November, after Rezko's October indictment. Obama, in response to questions from the press, termed the transactions related to his house "boneheaded." He said, "It was a mistake to have been engaged with him at all in this or any other personal business dealing that would allow him, or anyone else, to believe that he had done me a favor."

The candidate had not, however, done anything illegal. The issue faded. In March 2008, his 2010 U.S. Senate re-election campaign committee announced it would give the contributions by Rezko and his family members and associates to charity. In June, the developer was convicted on 16 counts of corruption and went to prison.

The second week of March 2008 brought a new crisis. ABC News announced on 13 March that it had reviewed videos sold in the lobby of Trinity Church and found they showed repeated denunciations of the United States by Reverend Wright. "The government gives them the drugs, builds bigger prisons, passes a three-strike law and then wants us to sing 'God Bless America.' No, no, no, God damn America, that's in the Bible for killing innocent people," he said in a 2003 sermon. The U.S., he said, should not have been surprised by the 9/11 attacks. "We bombed Nagasaki, and we nuked far more than the thousands in New York and the Pentagon, and we never batted an eye," he preached on 16 September 2001. Indeed, the former marine said, "We have supported state terrorism against the Palestinians and black South Africans, and now we are indignant because the stuff we have done overseas is now brought right back to our own front yards. America's chickens are coming home to roost." Obama said he was not present when Wright gave the sermons at issue.

The uproar that resulted dominated campaign coverage for days and might have derailed Obama's campaign because it cut to core issues of race, national identity, and politics. Instead, the candidate took advantage of the attention and spoke directly to these issues in an address titled "A More Perfect Union" that he delivered at the National Constitution Center in Philadelphia on 18 March. Wright's statements showed "a profoundly distorted view of this country," he said. Yet the former marine was also "a man who spoke to me about our obligations to love one another; to care for the sick and

59

lift up the poor." "I can no more disown him than I can my white grandmother—a woman who helped raise me, a woman who sacrificed again and again for me, a woman who loves me as much as she loves anything in this world, but a woman who once confessed her fear of black men who passed by her on the street, and who on more than one occasion has uttered racial or ethnic stereotypes that made me cringe," he said. "The profound mistake of Reverend Wright's sermons is not that he spoke about racism in our society. It's that he spoke as if our society was static; as if no progress has been made. But what we know—what we have seen—is that America can change," he added.

Finally, he said, "We have a choice in this country. We can accept a politics that breeds division, and conflict, and cynicism.... We can play Reverend Wright's sermons on every channel, every day and talk about them from now until the election, and make the only question in this campaign whether or not the American people think that I somehow believe or sympathize with his most offensive words. . . . Or, at this moment, in this election, we can come together and say, 'Not this time.' This time we want to talk about the crumbling schools that are stealing the future of black children and white children and Asian children and Hispanic children and Native American children.

This time we want to reject the cynicism that tells us that these kids can't learn; that those kids who don't look like us are somebody else's problem. The children of America are not those kids, they are our kids, and we will not let them fall behind in a 21st century economy. Not this time." The speech received a favorable reaction, and the storm abated.

April 11 produced "Bittergate." The HuffingtonPost.com website posted an explanation Obama gave at a private fundraiser in San Francisco of the challenges he faced with working-class voters in Pennsylvania and Indiana. "It's not surprising they get bitter," he said, referring to decades of constrained economic opportunities. "They cling to guns or religion or antipathy to people who aren't like them or anti-immigrant sentiment or anti-trade sentiment as a way to explain their frustrations." Clinton said the remarks were "not reflective of the values and beliefs of Americans." McCain said Obama showed "breathtaking" elitism. Obama challenged the accusations, and noted in response to the charge of elitism that he had been raised by a single mother who relied for a time on food stamps, but conceded he could have been more diplomatic.

The first meeting between the candidates in seven weeks took place on 16 April in Philadelphia, six days before the Pennsylvania primary, at a debate hosted by ABC News. Expectations for a substantive exchange were high. Instead, the hosts focused on superficialities such as whether the candidates would choose each other for vice president (they declined to say), how often Obama wore an American flag lapel pin (occasionally), and how well he knew Bill Ayers, a professor of education at the University of Illinois at Chicago. Ayers, now a "valued member of the Chicago community," according to its mayor Richard M. Daley, was a co-founder of the Weather Underground in 1970. The group declared war against the United States and took credit for bombing two dozen public buildings, including the Pentagon. It fell apart after an explosion destroyed a Greenwich Village townhouse where members were building a nail bomb, apparently to attack an officer's dance at Fort Dix in New Jersey; three were killed. Ayers subsequently spent a decade on the run until charges against him were dropped because of prosecutorial misconduct. In 1995, he organized an event at his Hyde Park home to introduce Obama to neighbors and friends, and donated $200 to Obama's state senate campaign. "The notion that somehow as a consequence of me knowing somebody who engaged in detestable acts 40 years ago, when I was eight years old, somehow reflects on me and my values, doesn't make much sense," Obama responded. "This kind of game, in which anybody who I know, regardless of how flimsy the relationship is, is somehow—somehow their ideas could be attributed to me—I think the American people are smarter than that," he added.

Clinton needed to win Pennsylvania by 20 percent or more to have a realistic chance to catch Obama, given the relatively small number of primaries that remained. She won by ten percent. A sense of inevitability grew around Obama's campaign.

The Wright storm flared anew on 28 April. The reverend did not follow the candidate's conciliatory lead in his Philadelphia address. Instead, in a speech at the National Press Club in Washington, D.C., he called his congregant insincere: "Politicians say what they say and do what they do because of electability," Wright said: "He had to distance himself because he's a politician." The pastor repeated assertions that the U.S. government may have introduced the AIDS virus into the African American community, and that the country might be responsible in part for the 9/11 attacks. Obama broke with the reverend the next day. He decried the address as "a bunch of rants that aren't grounded in the truth."

NATIONAL PRESS CLUB

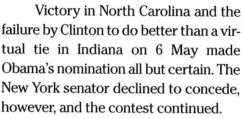

Victory in North Carolina and the failure by Clinton to do better than a virtual tie in Indiana on 6 May made Obama's nomination all but certain. The New York senator declined to concede, however, and the contest continued.

Trinity Church was back in the news on 25 May: a story that seemingly would not die. Michael Pfleger, the white pastor of a neighboring Chicago church and long-time acquaintance of Obama, mocked Senator Clinton from the pulpit during a guest sermon. "I really believe that she just always thought, 'This is mine. I'm Bill's wife, I'm white and this is mine. I just gotta get up and step into the plate.' And then out of nowhere came, 'Hey, I'm Barack Obama.' And she said, 'Oh, damn, where did you come from? I'm white. I'm entitled. There's a black man stealing my show.'" Obama resigned from the church, his spiritual home for two decades, a few days later. "We don't want to have to answer for everything that's stated in the church," he said.

The last hope for Clinton faded on 1 June when the Democratic Party's Rules Committee decided that delegates elected in Michigan and Florida would be seated at the convention—but would

MICHAEL PFLEGER

receive votes worth only one-half the regular amount as punishment for scheduling their primaries earlier than allowed by party rules. Obama was awarded all uncommitted Michigan delegates: since his name did not appear on the ballot, his campaign had urged supporters to vote "uncommitted." The 15-12 vote left Obama's delegate lead intact: 202 before the Rules Committee vote and 174 afterwards. Even if all the delegates had been granted a full vote, however, Obama still would have had more delegates than Clinton.

PRIMARIES IN DISPUTE

In what he said was, "a defining moment for our nation," Obama announced after polls closed on 3 June in South Dakota and Montana, the last two primary states, that he would be the Democratic nominee. He spoke to the nation from the St. Paul arena where the Republicans planned to hold their convention in September. The next day, he ordered the Democratic Party to stop taking money from lobbyists. On 7 June, Clinton conceded and endorsed Obama. "I ask all of you to join me in working as hard for Barack Obama as you have for me," she said to her supporters. To underscore the point, the two appeared together at the end of June in Unity, a tiny town in south-central New Hampshire where each received 107 votes in the primary.

Obama's primary campaign had raised over $295 million from approximately 1.5 million individuals. It was an unprecedented achievement, perhaps impossible before the Internet. Given the magnitude of this sum and predictions he could raise more from millions of fresh donors, Obama decided to reject $84 million in public funding for the general election. If he had taken it, he would have been barred from accepting additional contributions from individuals. "The public financing of presidential elections as it exists today is broken, and we face opponents who have become masters at gaming this broken system," he said in a statement. He was the first presidential candidate from a major party since Watergate to decline public funds. In *The Audacity of Hope*, he wrote, "Public financing of campaigns or free television and radio time could drastically reduce the constant scrounging for money and the influence of special interests." Now, he showed his practical side. McCain announced on the same day that his run would be publicly funded.

The pressure of the soaring ambitions Obama had unleashed for some in his campaign began to build. In an informal talk with his Chicago campaign staff in mid-June, he said, "We don't have an option now. When we were at the beginning of this thing in Iowa, if I lost Iowa, it would have been okay, you know? One of the other Democrats would have emerged and they would have carried the banner and we would have joined their campaign and we would have moved forward and the country would move in a better direction. But because we won, we now have no choice." We don't have a choice, he continued, "because now if we screw this up, all those people that I've met, who really need help, they're not going to get help. Those of you that are concerned about global warming, I don't care what John McCain says, he is not going to push that agenda. All those who are concerned about Darfur, I guarantee you they are not going to spend any political capital on that. Those of you who are concerned about education, there will be a bunch of lip service and then there will be more of the same. Those of you who are concerned about making sure that there's a sense of fairness in our economy, it will be less fair. So now everybody is counting on you, not just me, and I know that's a heavy weight but also what a magnificent position to find yourselves in, where the whole country is counting on you to change it for the better. Now those moments don't come around very often. And here you are, five months away from having transformed the country and made history and changed the world. So we've got to seize it, so rest up a little bit, but come back, ready to go . . . and fired up. I love you guys, let's go win the election."

6/11/08 —
6/25/08

V: CAMPAIGN FOR PRESIDENT, JUNE-NOVEMBER 2008

The general election campaign set Obama's call for change against John McCain's pledge to continue the policies of the Bush administration with respect to deregulation, tax cuts, and the war in Iraq. Obama led at the outset, fell behind after Alaska Governor Sarah Palin was nominated for Vice President at the end of August, then pulled ahead for good when the economy nosedived in the middle of September. A steady and disciplined campaign, continued Internet-based fund raising success, and strong turnout by his supporters ensured his historic victory in November.

June and July were all Obama. The candidate led national polls by about six points and had a convincing margin in electoral college projections. The constitution stipulates that each state get one electoral vote for each Representative and one for each Senator: 535, plus three for the District of Columbia, for a total of 538. Thus, 270 are required to be elected President. Every state, except Maine and Nebraska, uses a "winner-take-all" system that grants all of its electors to whichever candidate gets the most votes. Presidential campaigns thus focus their efforts on "swing" states, where polls show support is split and the final vote could go either way, to the exclusion of states where the outcome seems clear.

The Obama campaign worked feverishly, despite their lead, to prepare for the coming contest. On 12 June the web team launched FightTheSmears.com to centralize responses to future attacks. In the same month, volunteer coordinators recruited, trained and deployed 3,600 "Obama Organizing Fellows," each of whom had offered to work full-time for six weeks for free, to 17 swing states in what it called the largest grass-roots organizing effort in U.S. electoral history. Donors contributed $52 million in June, one of the Illinois senator's best months ever and more than double the $22 million raised by McCain.

The dynamic changed at the end of July when Obama made a whirlwind four-day tour of Kuwait, Afghanistan, Iraq, Jordan, the West Bank, Israel, Germany, France, and the United Kingdom. He capped the trip with a speech in Berlin to an estimated 200,000 cheering Germans.

The expedition initially seemed like a good idea. Obama had been to Iraq only once, and had never been to Afghanistan. McCain had criticized him for this parochialism, and sardonically offered to escort him to Kabul. In a *Washington Post*-ABC News poll released on 18 July, 72 percent of respondents said McCain knew enough about world affairs to be an effective president, compared to just 54 percent for Obama. The trip promised enormous coverage: dozens of top newspaper reporters and three of the network news anchors accompanied the frontrunner.

In practice, however, the overseas voyage created an opening for McCain. The Berlin crowd was the largest of the campaign. "People of Berlin—people of the world—this is our moment. This is our time," Obama said. McCain's reply was an ad released in Colorado, Iowa, Michigan, Missouri, Nevada, New Hampshire, New Mexico, Ohio, Pennsylvania, Virginia, and Wisconsin the following week that began, "He's the biggest celebrity in the world." The screen showed the Berlin rally, followed by images of Britney Spears and Paris Hilton. "But, is he ready to lead?" the voice-over continued. "With gas prices soaring, Barack Obama says no to offshore drilling. And, says he'll raise taxes on electricity. Higher taxes, more foreign oil, that's the real Obama," the spot concluded. Watchdog groups said the ad was false because Obama had not said he would raise taxes on electricity, but the idea of Obama as an immature egotist was planted. McCain hit the same theme when he hammered Obama for what he called a tentative response to an incursion into U.S. ally Georgia by Russia. Obama's poll numbers started to decline. McCain's rose.

The media attention Obama received, it emerged, was not always flattering. The Illinois senator got more than twice as much coverage on the CBS, ABC and NBC evening newscasts as his Arizona rival from mid-June to the end of July, analyst Andrew Tyndall reported—but it was more negative. A study by the Center for Media and Public Affairs at George Mason University found that when network newscasters ventured opinions during this period, 28 percent were positive for Obama and 72 percent were negative; by contrast, 43 percent of opinions were positive for McCain and 57 percent negative. A response to the "Celebrity" ad by Paris Hilton on 5 August in which she attacked "wrinkly, white-haired guy" McCain, "the oldest celebrity in the world"—"old enough to remember when dancing was a sin and beer was served in a bucket"— and declared her own candidacy for president ("I'm just hot") did little to change opinions.

The critical news coverage and negative advertisements co-incided with the release of two nationwide bestsellers that were harshly critical of Obama. Jerome Corsi's *The Obama Nation: Leftist Politics and the Cult of Personality*, an intentional play on the word "abomination," jumped to number one on the *New York Times* bestseller list, boosted by bulk purchases, on 1 August. The book alleged that Obama was corrupt, driven by "black rage," and possibly Muslim, among other charges. Corsi authored a similarly provocative attack against John Kerry called *Unfit for Command* in 2004 that received wide publicity and was perceived to have contributed to his defeat.

The Case Against Barack Obama: The Unlikely Rise and Un-examined Agenda of the Media's Favorite Candidate by David Freddoso, a reporter for the conservative *National Review* Online website, debuted on 4 August at number five on the *New York Times* bestseller list. Its ranking also was helped by bulk purchases. Freddoso alleged that Obama supported *de facto* infanticide because he voted against "Born Alive" bills in the Illinois state senate from 2001 to 2003; used his clout as a U.S. Senator to help save "the corrupt Cook County Political

Machine;" and had repeatedly steered taxpayer money to campaign donors, among other charges.

The Obama campaign responded on 15 August with both old and new techniques. First, a spokesperson commented, "These books are cut from the same cloth, made up of the same old debunked smears that have been floating around the Internet for months." Second, the campaign posted *Unfit for Publication*, a 22,000 word reply to Corsi's book packed with scathing reviews, detailed refutations of specific points, and background information about the author intended to undermine his credibility, on FightTheSmears.com. The title was a play on the author's 2004 book. Traditional media was interested in the point-counterpoint. They wrote some 1,060 stories about *The Obama Nation*, and cited *Unfit for Publication* about 670 times. Blogs were obsessed: they posted about 5,820 stories that cited the book, and 2,464 pieces that noted the campaign's rebuttal.

The attacks were effective. Obama's support fell at the beginning of August and remained flat through the middle of the month. McCain's popularity rose. Polls released just before the Democratic convention in Denver showed the frontrunner's lead had been cut in half, to about three percent nationwide.

The convention began unofficially on 23 August when Obama declared that Delaware Senator Joe Biden, a 36-year Congressional veteran with extensive foreign policy experience, would be his running mate. The news was released through a text message to supporters. The gimmick made a political point about new possibilities for direct communication, created additional media interest in the story, and allowed the campaign to collect mobile telephone numbers. Biden, "brings extensive foreign policy experience, an impressive record of collaborating across party lines, and a direct approach to getting the job done," Obama said. The choice of the veteran senator, a Catholic who grew up in the swing state of Pennsylvania, was seen as savvy and judicious by many. The McCain campaign, however, trumpeted criticisms of Obama made by Biden during the primary campaign. "Biden has denounced Barack Obama's poor foreign policy judgment and has strongly argued in his own words what Americans are quickly realizing—that Barack Obama is not ready to be President," a spokesman said.

The keynote speeches at the convention stressed themes of reconciliation and unity and attacked McCain as a continuation of the Bush-Cheney government. Michelle Obama made the first major address on 25 August. "He'll achieve these goals the same way he always has," she said of her husband. "By bringing us together and reminding us how much we share and how alike we really are. You see, Barack doesn't care where you're from, or what your background is, or what party—if any—you belong to. That's not how he sees the world. He knows that thread that connects us—our belief in America's promise, our commitment to our children's future. He knows that that thread is strong enough to hold us together as one nation even when we disagree," she added.

Senator Clinton spoke the next night. She laid to rest any concern that she might not wholeheartedly support Obama after the grueling primary contest—a subject of fevered speculation in the media. "No way, no how, no McCain," she began. She made an adroit reference to the historical nature of her candidacy as a woman, and her legions of female supporters: "To my supporters, my champions—my sisterhood of the traveling pantsuits—from the bottom of my heart: Thank you."

Finally, she tied Senator McCain to the deeply unpopular Bush administration—and linked Obama to the best accomplishments of her husband's presidency: "But we don't need four more years . . . of the last eight years. . . . When Barack Obama is in the White House, he'll revitalize our economy, defend the working people of America, and meet the global challenges of our time. Democrats know how to do this. As I recall, President Clinton and the Democrats did it before. And President Obama and the Democrats will do it again," she said. Former President Clinton echoed these themes the next night. "He has a remarkable ability to inspire people, to raise our hopes and rally us to high purpose. He has the intelligence and curiosity every successful president needs," he said of Obama.

Finally, on the last night of the convention, Obama accepted the party's nomination before a thunderous crowd of 84,000 at Denver's Mile High Stadium. He tied McCain to Bush; attacked him for excessive devotion to individualism in contrast to his own affirmation of community; reviewed a list of policy specifics; and closed with a call for rededication to individual and collective responsibilities. "The record's clear: John McCain has voted with George Bush ninety percent of the time. Senator McCain likes to talk about judgment, but really, what does it say about your judgment when you think George Bush has been right more than ninety percent of the time? I don't know about you, but I'm not ready to take a ten percent chance on change," he said.

"For over two decades, he's subscribed to that old, discredited Republican philosophy—give more and more to those with the most and hope that prosperity trickles down to everyone else. In Washington, they call this the Ownership Society, but what it really means is—you're on your own. Out of work? Tough luck. No health care? The market will fix it. Born into poverty? Pull yourself up by your own bootstraps—even if you don't have boots. You're on your own," he continued. By contrast, he said, the promise of America is, "The idea that we are responsible for ourselves, but that we also rise or fall as one nation; the fundamental belief that I am my brother's keeper; I am my sister's keeper."

"America, now is not the time for small plans," Obama said, as he outlined his proposals for reform of virtually every sector of the economy, from energy to education and health care to Social Security.

Finally, he said, "We must also admit that fulfilling America's promise will require more than just money. It will require a renewed sense of responsibility from each of us to recover what John F. Kennedy called our 'intellectual and moral strength.' Yes, government must lead on energy independence, but each of us must do our part to make our homes and businesses more efficient. Yes, we must provide more ladders to success for young men who fall into lives of crime and despair. But we must also admit that programs alone can't replace parents; that government can't turn off the television and make a child do her homework; that fathers must take more responsibility for providing the love and guidance their children need. Individual responsibility and mutual responsibility—that's the essence of America's promise," he concluded.

The next day John McCain dropped a bombshell that tore the country's attention away from Obama and gave the Republican the lead for the first time: he selected Sarah Palin, the relatively unknown 44-year-old governor of Alaska for two years, as his running mate. Palin's only significant government experience before becoming governor had been as Mayor of the town of Wasilla, population about 5,500 at the time, for six years, and a member of its city council for four years before that. "She's not from these parts, and she's not from Washington, but when you get to know her, you're going to be as impressed as I am," McCain told 15,000 people in a basketball arena in Dayton, Ohio when he made the announcement.

Republicans initially applauded the selection. Palin was an evangelical Christian, hunter, happily married wife and mother of five, and the first woman nominee for Vice President in party history. Enthusiasm spread after her speech to a television audience estimated at 37 million—nearly as many as tuned in for Obama's acceptance speech—at the Republican convention in St. Paul, Minnesota the following week.

She was, she said, a hockey mom: "You know [what], they say the difference [is] between a hockey mom and a pit bull? Lipstick." She mocked Obama and the news media. "I guess a small-town mayor is sort of like a community organizer, except that you have actual responsibilities," she said. "Here's a little newsflash for those reporters and commentators: I'm not going to Washington to seek their good opinion. I'm going to Washington to serve the people of this great country," she added. She praised people from small towns: "I grew up with those people. They're the ones who do some of the hardest work in America, who grow our food, and run our factories, and fight our wars. They love their country in good times and bad, and they're always proud of America." She proposed new drilling for oil and gas to chants of "Drill, baby, drill!" and a renewed commitment to the Iraq war; promised lower taxes and spending; and presented her administration as defined by simple tastes and frugality. "I got rid of a few things in the governor's office that I didn't believe our citizens should have to pay for. That luxury jet was over-the-top. I put it on eBay," she said. "I told the Congress, 'Thanks, but no thanks,' on that Bridge to Nowhere," she added, referring to a plan to build a $398 million bridge with federal funds to an island with population of 50 full-time residents and a small airport. "This lady has turned it all around . . . from now on, on this program John McCain will be known as John McBrilliant," conservative radio talk show host Rush Limbaugh said the next day.

McCain continued the themes of lower taxes and spending, more drilling, and an unwavering commitment to the war in Iraq when he accepted the nomination the next night. "I will cut government spending. He will increase it. My tax cuts will create jobs; his tax increases will eliminate them," he said. "We will drill new wells off-shore, and we'll drill them now," he continued. "I've fought for the right strategy and more troops in Iraq when it wasn't the popular thing to do. . . . I'd rather lose an election than see my country lose," he declared. Finally, he stressed his experience. "I have that record and the scars to prove it. Senator Obama does not," he said.

The speeches resonated. Support for Obama in averages of multiple national polls peaked at around 47 percent at the end of August just before the Democratic convention, stayed flat though the end of the month, then dropped during and immediately after the Republican confab to about 45 percent. Enthusiasm for McCain jumped from about 44 percent at the end of August to about 46 percent in the first week of September.

The Republican surge was short-lived. On 7 September Fannie Mae, the Federal National Mortgage Association, and Freddie Mac, the Federal Home Loan Mortgage Corporation, private firms supported by an implicit government guarantee that underwrote many of the nation's home mortgages, became insolvent and were taken over by the government. On 14 September the Wall Street investment bank Lehman Brothers declared the largest bankruptcy in U.S. history. Its debts were larger than the gross domestic product of Poland. On the same day, Bank of America acquired brokerage firm Merrill Lynch in a forced sale brokered by the government. Thousands of jobs were lost. Commentators compared the crisis to the Depression of the 1930s. The polls reversed almost immediately: Obama's numbers began to rise, and McCain's to fall.

McCain's first public response to the economic crisis was a speech in Jacksonville Florida on 15 September at which he said, "The fundamentals of our economy are strong." Obama responded immediately: "It's not that I think John McCain doesn't care [about] what's going on in the lives of most Americans. I just think he doesn't know. Why else would he say, today, of all days, just a few hours ago, that the fundamentals of our economy are strong? Senator, what economy are you talking about?" McCain later claimed that by "fundamentals" he meant American workers.

The crisis continued to worsen in the third week of September, just six weeks from election day. On the 24th, McCain said he had suspended his campaign, asked Obama to postpone the first debate scheduled for three days later, and flew to Washington, D.C. to help negotiate a $700 billion financial rescue plan proposed by Treasury Secretary Henry Paulson. Obama refused to delay the debate. "It's my belief that this is exactly the time when the American people need to hear from the person who will be the next president," he said. "It is going to be part of the president's job to deal with more than one thing at once," he added. On Thursday the 25th, Washington Mutual Savings Bank collapsed—the largest bank failure in U.S. history—and a White House meeting between President Bush and Republican and Democratic leaders, including Obama and McCain, to discuss Paulson's proposal broke up in acrimony. The breakdown of discussions, despite McCain's high-profile rush back to the capital, combined with the fact that his campaign kept its offices open and continued to advertise during the "suspension" made the senator and his team appear hapless and erratic. Obama, by contrast, was unflappable in interviews. His campaign conducted business as usual.

McCain's campaign was damaged by two additional setbacks during the week. On the 23rd, it emerged that Freddie Mac paid $15,000 a month from the end of 2005 through August 2008—the total was ultimately shown to be more than $2 million—to a lobbying firm owned by McCain campaign manager Rick Davis. The next day McCain's staff, perhaps confused by the sudden "suspension" announcement, double-booked the candidate for appearances on CBS News with Katie Couric and The Late Show with David Letterman. McCain, a frequent guest on Letterman's show, cancelled with apologies that he had to return immediately to Washington. Shortly thereafter, however, the talk show host's staff observed him on a live satellite feed from the CBS studios, a few blocks from their own building in Manhattan, getting ready to appear on Couric's program. Letterman relayed the CBS feed live on his program and unleashed a torrent of invective. "You don't suspend your campaign. This doesn't smell right. This isn't the way a tested hero behaves . . . I think someone's putting something in his Metamucil," he said. He pummeled McCain relentlessly through November.

The first presidential debate, focused on foreign policy and national security, took place on 27 September at the University of Mississippi. Discussion quickly turned to the economic crisis: a global matter that affected security. Obama was decisive. "This is a final verdict on eight years of failed economic policies—promoted by George Bush, supported by Sen. McCain . . . a theory that basically says that we can shred regulations and consumer protections and give more and more to the most, and somehow, prosperity will trickle down," he said, in an echo of his convention acceptance speech. "It hasn't worked," he continued, "and I think that the fundamentals of the economy have to be measured by whether or not the middle class is getting a fair shake. That's why I'm running for president." McCain responded that if he were elected president he would focus first on elimination of pork barrel spending. "I've got a pen and I'm going to veto every spending bill that comes across my desk," he said. In fact, however, as commenters quickly noted, pork barrel projects, while problematic, were a tiny fraction of the overall budget and were not believed to have played a significant role in the crisis.

Obama also attacked on the subject of Iraq. "We've spent over $600 billion so far, soon to be $1 trillion," Obama said. "We have lost over 4,000 lives. We have seen 30,000 wounded, and most importantly, from a strategic national security perspective, al Qaeda is resurgent, stronger now than at any time since 2001." "We took our eye off the ball," he added, "and not to mention that we are still spending $10 billion a month when they [Iraqis] have a $79 billion surplus, at a time when we are in great distress here at home." A national poll of viewers by CNN immediately after the event judged Obama the winner 51 percent to 38 percent.

The House rejected Paulson's plan two days later by a vote of 228-205. Republicans led the opposition and voted 133-65 against the plan. Democrats voted 140-95 in favor. The Dow Industrial Average stock index fell 777 points in response: its worst single-day drop in two decades. McCain's poll numbers declined in lock step.

Palin's appeal also was in decline. First, her convention speech claims that she put the state plane "on eBay," and said "Thanks, but no thanks," to the federal government about the "Bridge to Nowhere," did not withstand scrutiny. The jet was listed on eBay but didn't sell.

The state finally sold it to a local businessman at a loss of almost $600,000. The record also showed that she actually supported the "Bridge to Nowhere," and its pork-barrel federal financing, during her 2006 run for governor.

Second, interviews with ABC News anchor Charlie Gibson on 11 September and CBS News anchor Katie Couric on 24 September raised questions about her preparation to be chief executive. In her interview with Gibson, she asserted that Russia's proximity to Alaska—"You can actually see Russia from land here in Alaska,"—gave her insight into bilateral relations. She also appeared not to know what the Bush Doctrine was (the doctrine, announced after the 9/11 attacks, asserted that the U.S. could attack other countries preemptively to protect itself). In her interview with Couric, her answer to a question about Paulson's debt relief plan suggested she didn't fully understand the issue. "I'm all about the position that America is in and that we have to look at a $700 billion bailout. And as Sen. McCain has said unless this nearly trillion dollar bailout is what it may end up to be, unless there are amendments in Paulson's proposal, really I don't believe that Americans are going to support this and we will not support this," she said. She insisted that McCain had long supported additional regulation of the financial system, but couldn't cite any examples. "I'll try to find you some and I'll bring them to you," she told the journalist.

The Vice-Presidential debate on 2 October generated enormous interest—over 70 million people watched, far more than tuned in to the presidential debate—but did not help Palin. Post-debate polling deemed Biden the winner 51 percent to 36 percent. Mainstream conservatives were harsh in their criticisms. "If BS were currency, Palin could bail out Wall Street herself," Kathleen Parker wrote in the *National Review Online*.

Her anti-intellectualism is "a fatal cancer to the Republican party," said *New York Times* columnist David Brooks. "What on earth can he have been thinking?" Christopher Buckley wondered of McCain.

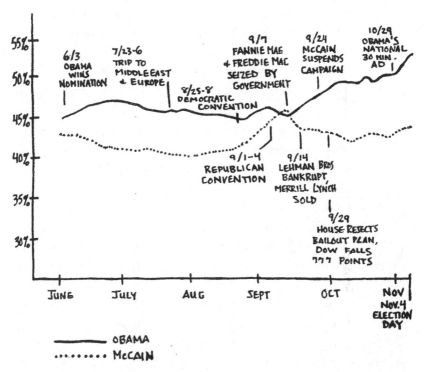

NATIONAL OPINION POLLS   JUNE 1ST – NOV. 4

As the race entered its final month, Obama's lead in national polls had widened to about seven points. This matched the largest margin of the campaign and returned the race to where it had been in mid-July. Projections showed the Democrat well ahead in the electoral college. Particularly worrisome for the McCain campaign was the fact that their numbers had been in decline since their convention. They sharpened their attack. Palin led the charge. At a rally on 5 October she cited Bill Ayers and described Obama as "someone who sees America, it seems, as being so imperfect that he's palling around with terrorists who would target their own country." She repeated the incendiary allegation at subsequent events. Supporters responded. Videos of Palin's subsequent rallies posted on YouTube recorded shouts of "Treason!", "Off with his head!", "He is a bomb!" and, in one instance, "Kill him," although it was not clear if the comment was aimed at Obama or at Ayers. The governor, although she paused on occasion, did not challenge the statements. She later called the threats "atrocious and unacceptable," and said she hadn't heard them.

The second presidential debate continued the focus of the first on economic issues. McCain announced a new proposal to spend $300 billion to buy back bad mortgages from banks—but was vague about the details. His eyes were red and he looked tired. He appeared unwilling to look directly at his opponent and, toward the end of the contest, referred to him awkwardly as "that one." Obama offered no new proposals, but seemed at ease and collected. CNN's post-event survey scored the exchange 54 percent for Obama to 30 percent for McCain.

Criticism of Palin mounted on 10 October when a bipartisan panel formed by the Alaska legislature to investigate a controversy dubbed Troopergate concluded she "unlawfully abused her power as governor by trying to have her former brother-in-law fired as a state trooper." The governor herself, however, categorically dismissed the finding. "Well, I'm very, very pleased to be cleared of any legal wrongdoing . . . any hint of any kind of unethical activity there," she said.

Perhaps mindful of the Troopergate report, or concerned by information from the Secret Service about an increase in threats to Obama in September and early October, McCain signaled the same day that he wanted to scale back the attacks. "If you want a fight, we will fight," he said at a rally in Minnesota. "But we will be respectful. I admire Senator Obama and his accomplishments. I will respect him, and I want—no, no," McCain said over boos, "I want everyone to be respectful." The candidate corrected a woman who said Obama was "an Arab." "No. No, ma'am. No, ma'am. No, ma'am. No, ma'am," McCain said, "He's a decent family man, a citizen, that I just happen to have disagreements with on fundamental issues; that's what this campaign is about." It later emerged that McCain had decided at the beginning of the campaign to avoid attacks based on the Reverend Wright, Michelle Obama, or Obama's lack of military service.

Ayers and the community group ACORN, however, were considered worthy subjects for discussion. McCain made them a central focus of his argument in the final debate on 15 October. "We need to know the full extent of that [Ayers] relationship. We need to know the full extent of Sen. Obama's relationship with ACORN, who is now on the verge of maybe perpetrating one of the greatest frauds in voter history in this country, maybe destroying the fabric of democracy," the Arizona senator said. Obama countered, "Mr. Ayers has become the centerpiece of McCain's campaign. Let's get the record straight. Ayers is a professor of education in Chicago. Forty years ago, when I was eight years old, he engaged in despicable acts. I have roundly condemned those acts." He served on a board with Ayers, he added—along with a former ambassador and the presidents of the University of Illinois and Northwestern University. His only involvement with ACORN, he said, was to help represent them "alongside the U.S. Justice Department" to force Illinois to implement a law to allow people to register to vote at Department of Motor Vehicles offices.

McCain also spent a considerable period of time discussing a man he dubbed "Joe the Plumber" who had confronted Obama while the candidate campaigned in Toledo, Ohio the week before. "Joe wants to buy the business that he has been in for all of these years, worked 10, 12 hours a day. And he wanted to buy the business but he looked at your tax plan and he saw that he was going to pay much higher taxes," McCain said. Obama repied, "I think tax policy is a major difference between Senator McCain and myself. And we both want to cut taxes, the difference is who we want to cut taxes for. Now, Senator McCain, the centerpiece of his economic proposal is to provide $200 billion in additional tax breaks to some of the wealthiest corporations in America. . . . What I've said is I want to provide a tax cut for 95 percent of working Americans." Viewers found Obama's arguments more convincing: CNN's post-debate survey scored the contest 58-31 for the Illinois senator, the widest margin of the three face-offs. McCain's arguments was further undercut when it later emerged that Joe was not a licensed plumber, had a lien against him by the state of Ohio for unpaid taxes, and made so much less money than he claimed that he likely would have received a tax cut under Obama's plan.

An air of inevitability began to surround Obama's candidacy when retired General Colin Powell, a former Chairman of the Joint Chiefs of Staff under President George H. W. Bush and Secretary of State for George W. Bush, and himself a possible Republican presidential candidate, endorsed him on 19 October.

"I don't believe [Palin] is ready to be president of the United States," he said. Powell added he was "troubled" by the personal attacks on Obama, especially intimations he might be Muslim, because they were untrue and because there was no reason a Muslim-American shouldn't seek the presidency. "Is there something wrong with being a Muslim in this country? The answer's no, that's not America," he said. "I feel strongly about this particular point because of a picture I saw . . . of a mother in Arlington Cemetery, and she had her head on the headstone of her son's grave. . . . it had [the] crescent and a star of the Islamic faith. And his name was

Kareem Rashad Sultan Khan, and he was an American. He was born in New Jersey. He was 14 years old at the time of 9/11, and he waited until he can go serve his country, and he gave his life. Now, we have got to stop polarizing ourself in this way," he continued. The focus on Ayers, he thought, was inappropriate given the scant contact between the candidate and the professor. Finally, he said he was concerned about McCain's apparent lack of understanding about how to deal with economic problems. "I truly believe that at this point in America's history we need a president who will not just continue . . . basically the policies we have followed in recent years," Powell said. "We need a president with transformational qualities."

On the day of Powell's endorsement, the Obama campaign announced it had added 632,000 new donors and raised over $150 million in September. The average donation for the month was less than $100. The total number of donors was now over three million people. On 23 October, NBC announced that Obama's lead had grown to 52 to 42 percent, up from 49 to 43 percent two weeks before, and the largest margin of the campaign.

Bad news continued for McCain. The website Politico.com reported on 22 October that the Republican National Committee had spent over $150,000 on Palin's wardrobe since her nomination, including between $20,000 and $40,000 on clothes for her husband. Low-level staffers had been required to use their credit cards to pay for some items. Palin's representatives said many of the clothes had been purchased in multiple sizes. Unused garments had been returned. All of the items would be given to charity after the election, they said. The spending nonetheless appeared extravagant to many.

Polls now showed that Palin, despite her ability to draw large crowds of fervent supporters at rallies, had become McCain's greatest liability. "Palin's qualifications to be president rank as voters' top concern about McCain's candidacy—ahead of continuing President Bush's policies, enacting economic policies that only benefit the rich and keeping too high of a troop presence in Iraq," NBC reported. "For the first time, more voters have a negative opinion of her than a positive one," the network added.

The campaign entered its endgame. Obama flew home to Hawaii to say farewell to his gravely ill grandmother from 23 to 25 October. On 29 October, his team bought a half-hour of prime airtime for an "Obama infomercial," as he called it. The $4 million closing argument, the first time a presidential candidate had purchased a large block of network prime time since Ross Perot in 1992, told the stories of four voters, their families, and challenges they faced. Obama offered details about his housing, tax, energy and Iraq war policies in interludes between the documentaries. The promotion ended with live footage of the candidate at a late-night rally for 20,000 people at Sunrise, Florida. Nielsen reported 33.6 million people watched the program. Even later that night,

Obama appeared for the first time with former president Bill Clinton at a rally of 35,000 people at Kissimmee, Florida.

The Obama campaign unleashed a barrage of advertising in the days leading up to 4 November, and a get out of the vote operation on Election Day unlike anything ever seen in U.S. politics. In addition to an avalanche of television commercials in swing states, the team's efforts included a dedicated 24-hour satellite channel that showed nothing but speeches by Obama and promotions for him, commercials inserted in video games, and dozens of daily uploads to YouTube and other Internet distribution channels. The campaign mobilized tens of thousands of volunteers, coordinated by hundreds of field offices, to ensure that supporters— identified by painstaking door-to-door and telephone canvasses prior to Election Day—actually voted. An army of thousands of attorneys recruited by the campaign's Counsel for Change voter protection program stood watch at polling places to ensure that every eligible supporter was allowed to vote.

The McCain campaign tried to match Obama's effort. The Republicans countered the Democrat ad-for-ad in key battleground states such as Florida, Ohio, North Carolina, Virginia, and Pennsylvania in the last days of the race. It also mounted its own nationwide "72 hour program" in the days just before the election to get out the vote. The Republican National Committee reported 5.4 million voter contacts in the week before the election, although many were automated telephone "robo-calls" rather than personal visits, compared with 1.9 million in the same week in 2004. McCain appeared at 252 events in battleground states during the general election and Palin at 150, compared to 230 appearances for Obama and 107 for Biden.

In the final analysis, however, Obama's outreach was significantly greater than McCain's. The Democrat spent $593.1 million from the beginning of his primary campaign through 4 November, compared to $273.5 million for his rival. Obama ran about 370,000 television advertisements in the general election, compared to around 250,000 by McCain. The Republican National Committee spent $36 million for an additional approximately 71,000 spots, but the differential still was substantial. Reports from Ohio after the election gave an indication of the comparative reach of the campaigns: 53 percent of voters said they had been personally contacted by the Obama team, compared to 36 percent who reported similar contact from McCain's campaign.

Election Day began auspiciously for Obama: he won the New Hampshire hamlets of Dixville Notch and Hart's Location, the first places in the country to announce results, by votes of 15-6 and 17-10, respectively. The two candidates voted in their home states, then spent the day at last-minute rallies as their teams swung into action at polls across the country.

Pennsylvania was the first major battleground state to be called for Obama. When Ohio followed a bit later in the evening, the math was clear. It wasn't until polls closed on the West Coast at 11:00 p.m. eastern time, however, that news organizations declared Obama victorious. Supporters spilled into the streets of major cities. They danced in Harlem, tooted horns in Boston, cheered in Chicago, rejoiced in Atlanta and sang in San Francisco and Seattle, among many other scenes of jubilation. More than 1,000 celebrants shouted "Yes we can!" outside the White House.

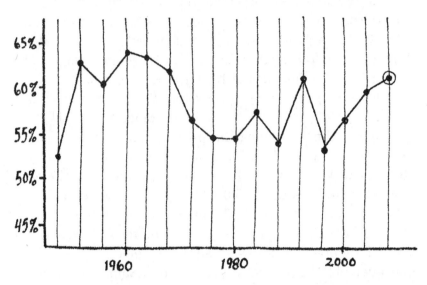

The first African American elected president received 66,882,230 votes, 53 percent of the total, to McCain's 58,343,671 or 46 percent. He won 365 of 538 electoral votes. It was the biggest Democratic victory since Lyndon Johnson in 1964, the first time a Democrat had won more than half of all votes since Jimmy Carter in 1976, and the first time a Democrat won a majority of male voters since Bill Clinton in 1996.

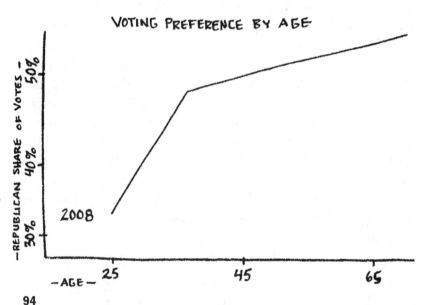

VOTING PREFERENCE BY AGE

RESULTS BY STATE

▦ **OBAMA**

☐ **McCAIN**

Obama won states that for many years had been reliably Republican, including Indiana and Virginia, neither of which had voted for a Democrat for president since Johnson. He won 68 percent of new voters, two-thirds of voters aged 18 to 29, 95 percent of blacks, 66 percent of Latinos, 54 percent of Catholics and a majority of independents and the rich: voters with incomes over $200,000. He did not win a majority of

VOTING SHIFTS FROM 2004 BY COUNTY (WEIGHTED FOR POPULATION)

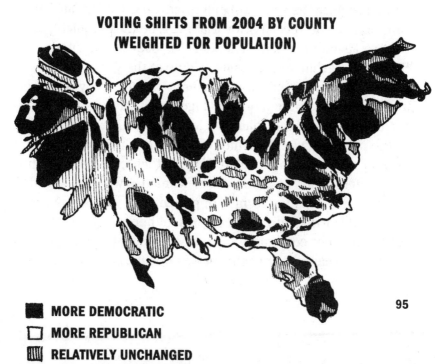

■ **MORE DEMOCRATIC**

☐ **MORE REPUBLICAN**

▥ **RELATIVELY UNCHANGED**

95

white voters, or those aged 65 and older. A record 127.5 million people voted, about 61 percent of eligible voters. It was the largest turnout in history in absolute numbers, but almost unchanged in percentage terms from the previous election.

In a testament to the effectiveness of the Obama campaign's get out the vote effort, Democratic turnout increased 2.6 points from 28.7 percent of voters in 2004 to 31.3 percent, while Republican turnout declined by 1.3 percentage points to 28.7 percent. The "blue," or Democratic, shift was nationwide, except for a band of counties in the deep south and along the southern portion of the Appalachian mountains where a larger "red" percentage voted for McCain than had voted for Bush in 2004. Democrats gained significant numbers of seats in the House and Senate and took firm control of both houses.

McCain was gracious in his concession speech. Of Obama he said, "In a contest as long and difficult as this campaign has been, his success alone commands my respect for his ability and perseverance. But that he managed to do so by inspiring the hopes of so many millions of Americans who had once wrongly believed that they had little at stake or little influence in the election of an American president is something I deeply admire and commend him for achieving." He continued, "This is an historic election, and I recognize the special significance it has for African Americans and for the special pride that must be theirs tonight. . . . A century ago, President Theodore Roosevelt's invitation of Booker T. Washington to visit—to dine at the White House was taken as an outrage in many quarters. America today is a world away from the cruel and prideful bigotry of that time. There is no better evidence of this than the election of an African American to the presidency of the United States. Let there be no reason now for any American to fail to cherish their citizenship in this, the greatest nation on Earth." He concluded, "I wish Godspeed to the man who was my former opponent and will be my president." Palin arrived prepared to present her own address, even though it is not customary for a vice-presidential candidate to deliver a concession speech, but was not allowed to talk.

Obama strode onto an outdoor stage in Chicago's Grant Park, named for the Union general who won the Civil War that ended slavery, just before midnight. An exultant crowd estimated at 240,000 cheered. His family joined him. "If there is anyone out there who still doubts that America is a place where all things are possible; who still wonders if the dream of our founders is alive in our time; who still questions the power of our democracy, tonight is your answer," he said.

"It's the answer told by lines that stretched around schools and churches in numbers this nation has never seen; by people who waited three hours and four hours, many for the very first time in their lives, because they believed that this time must be different; that their voice could be that difference. It's the answer spoken by young and old, rich and poor, Democrat and Republican, black, white, Latino, Asian, Native American, gay, straight, disabled and not disabled—Americans who sent a message to the world that we have never been a collection of red states and blue states: we are, and always will be, the United States of America. It's the answer that led those who have been told for so long by so many to be cynical, and fearful, and doubtful of what we can achieve, to put their hands on the arc of history and bend it once more toward the hope of a better day. It's been a long time coming, but tonight, because of what we did on this day, in this election, at this defining moment, change has come to America," he continued.

The change that had happened, however, was only a chance, he said, for the change his campaign sought: "This victory alone is not the change we seek—it is only the chance for us to make that change. And that cannot happen if we go back to the way things were. It cannot happen without you. . . . The road ahead will be long. Our climb will be steep. We may

not get there in one year or even one term, but America—I have never been more hopeful than I am tonight that we will get there. I promise you—we as a people will get there."

He told the story of Ann Nixon Cooper, a 106-year-old woman born one generation after slavery who voted that day in Atlanta. "She was born just a generation past slavery; a time when there were no cars on the road or planes in the sky; when someone like her couldn't vote for two reasons—because she was a woman and because of the color of her skin," he said. "And tonight, I think about all that she's seen throughout her century in America—the heartache and the hope; the struggle and the progress; the times we were told that we can't, and the people who pressed on with that American creed: Yes we can. At a time when women's voices were silenced and their hopes dismissed, she lived to see them stand up and speak out and reach for the ballot. Yes we can. When there was despair in the dust bowl and depression across the land, she saw a nation conquer fear itself with a New Deal, new jobs and a new sense of common purpose. Yes we can. When the bombs fell on our harbor and tyranny threatened the world, she was there to witness a generation rise to greatness and a democracy was saved. Yes we can. She was there for the buses in Montgomery, the hoses in Birmingham, a bridge in Selma, and a preacher from Atlanta who told a people that we shall overcome. Yes we can. A man touched down on the moon, a wall came down in Berlin, a world was connected by our own science and imagination. And this year, in this election, she touched her finger to a screen, and cast her vote, because after 106 years in America, through the best of times and the darkest of hours, she knows how America can change. Yes we can," he continued.

To rolling roars of approval and tear-stained faces he thanked his campaign team (the best "ever assembled in the history of politics"), his parents and grandparents, brothers and sisters, his wife ("the nation's next first lady"), and his daughters. "Sasha and Malia I love you both more than you can imagine. And you have earned the new puppy that's coming with us to the new White House," he said.

He concluded, "America, we have come so far. We have seen so much. But there is so much more to do. So tonight, let us ask ourselves—if our children should live to see the next century; if my daughters should be so lucky to live as long as Ann Nixon Cooper, what change will they see? What progress will we have made?"

NOTES

p. 1   *We … what works* Barack Obama. *The Audacity of Hope: Thoughts on Reclaiming the American Dream.* 2006 rpt. 2008: Vintage. 159.

p. 2   *following the war* Barack Obama. *Dreams from My Father: A Story of Race and Inheritance.* 1995 rev. 2004: Three Rivers Press. 407.

innocent and released Ben Macintyre and Paul Orengoh. "Beatings and abuse made Barack Obama's grandfather loathe the British: The President-elect's relatives have told how the family was a victim of the Mau Mau revolt." 3 December 2008: TimesOnline.co.uk. Accessed 3 December 2008.

Habiba Akumu John Oywa. "Kenya: Special Report: Sleepy Little Village Where Obama Traces His Own Roots." 15 August 2004: The Nation. Accessed 13 July 2008.

Xan Rice. "Barack's voice was just like his father's — I thought he had come back from the dead." 6 June 2008: Guardian.co.uk.

two children and little money Obama. *Dreams from My Father.* 418-20.

son has written Barack Obama, "My Spiritual Journey." 16 October 2006. Time.com. See *Audacity of Hope*, 204.

never a muslim Xan Rice. 'Barack's voice was just like his father's — I thought he had come back from the dead.' 6 June 2008: Guardian.co.uk.

p. 3   *big bands* Tim Jones. "Barack Obama: Mother not just a girl from Kansas: Stanley Ann Dunham shaped a future senator." 27 March 2007: ChicagoTribune.com. Accessed 24 June 2008.

legs off a couch Tim Jones. "Barack Obama: Mother not just a girl from Kansas: Stanley Ann Dunham shaped a future senator." 27 March 2007: ChicagoTribune.com. Accessed 24 June 2008.

railroad tracks Tim Jones. "Barack Obama: Mother not just a girl from Kansas: Stanley Ann Dunham shaped a future senator." 27 March 2007: ChicagoTribune.com. Accessed 24 June 2008.

Harry S. Truman Scott Fornek. "Mareen Duvall: 'No more striking figure.' 9 September 2007: SunTimes.com. Accessed 24 June 2008.

received her diploma Tim Jones. "Barack Obama: Mother not just a girl from Kansas: Stanley Ann Dunham shaped a future senator." 27 March 2007: ChicagoTribune.com. Accessed 24 June 2008.

George S. Patton Obama. *Dreams from My Father.* 15.

grieved the girl Tim Jones. "Barack Obama: Mother not just a girl from Kansas: Stanley Ann Dunham shaped a future senator." 27 March 2007: ChicagoTribune.com. Accessed 24 June 2008. Madelyn's brother Charlie also served during the war and liberated Ohrdruf, a part of the Buchenwald death camp complex, a fact that became a minor issue during the Obama Presidential campaign. Christopher Wills. "Obama mistaken on name of Nazi death camp: Campaign says Obama made mistake in saying great-uncle helped liberate Nazi camp at Auschwitz." 28 May 2008: Newsweek.com. Accessed 24 June 2008.

East Shore Unitarian Church Tim Jones. "Barack Obama: Mother not just a girl from Kansas: Stanley Ann Dunham shaped a future senator." 27 March 2007: ChicagoTribune.com. Accessed 24 June 2008.

1984 Tim Jones. "Barack Obama: Mother not just a girl from Kansas: Stanley Ann Dunham shaped a future senator." 27 March 2007: ChicagoTribune.com. Accessed 24 June 2008. For the use of "Stanley Ann" see Amanda Ripley, "The Story of Barack Obama's Mother," 9 April 2008: Time.com.

too young to go Amanda Ripley. "The Story of Barack Obama's Mother." 9 April 2008: Time.com. See Obama, *Dreams from My Father,* 16.

University of Hawaii Obama. *Dreams from My Father.* 55.

p. 4   *told her he was divorced* David Mendell. Obama. *Obama: From Promise to Power.* 2007: Amistad. 30.

participated in the meetings Tim Jones. "Barack Obama: Mother not just a girl from Kansas: Stanley Ann Dunham shaped a future senator." 27 March 2007: ChicagoTribune.com. Accessed 24 June 2008.

white as milk Obama, *Dreams from My Father*. 10.

illegal in 22 states Kevin Merida, "The Ghost of a Father," 14 December 2007: Washington-Post.com.

dropped out of college Amanda Ripley. "The Story of Barack Obama's Mother," 9 April 2008: Time.com.

completed his studies Kevin Merida, "The Ghost of a Father," 14 December 2007: WashingtonPost.com.

Cambridge Obama, *Dreams from My Father*. 10.

p. 5   *filed for divorce* Amanda Ripley. "The Story of Barack Obama's Mother," 9 April 2008: Time.com.

was impressed nonetheless Obama. *The Audacity of Hope*. 274.

Franciscus Assisi Primary School Amanda Ripley. "The Story of Barack Obama's Mother," 9 April 2008: Time.com.

at the U.S. embassy Obama. *Dreams from My Father*. 36-7

p. 6   *car and driver* Obama. *The Audacity of Hope*. 275.

President Suharto Associated Press. "Obama debunks claim about Islamic school: Calls the reports 'scurrilous'; Jakarta school open to all faiths." 25 January 2007: MSNBC.MSN.com. Accessed 22 June 2008.

the only foreigner Amanda Ripley. "The Story of Barack Obama's Mother," 9 April 2008: Time.com. Accessed 22 June 2008.

two hours each week Paul Watson. "Islam an unknown factor in Obama bid: Campaign downplays his connection during boyhood in Indonesia." 16 March 2007: BaltimoreSun.com. Accessed 25 June 2008.

My mother ... transitory nature Obama. *The Audacity of Hope*. 205.

together at twilight Obama. *The Audacity of Hope*. 205.

But she had ... so did I Amanda Ripley. "The Story of Barack Obama's Mother," 9 April 2008: Time.com. Accessed 22 June 2008.

not devout Kim Barker, "Obama madrassa myth debunked," 25 March: ChicagoTribune.com. Accessed 22 June 2008.

never been a practicing Muslim Associated Press. "Obama debunks claim about Islamic school: Calls the reports 'scurrilous'; Jakarta school open to all faiths." 25 January 2007: Msnbc.msn.com. Accessed 22 June 2008.

The face ... by the wind. Obama. *Dreams from My Father*. 37.

p. 7   *She had learned ... lay elsewhere* Obama. *Dreams from My Father*. 47.

She came into ... buster Obama. *Dreams from My Father*. 48.

If you ... judgment Obama. *Dreams from My Father*. 49

In a land ... liberalism Obama. *Dreams from My Father*. 50.

p. 8   *My hands ... how does that feel* Obama. *Dreams from My Father*. 36,

The strong man ... Always Obama. *Dreams from My Father*. 4

p. 9   *$15,725 a year* Punahou School. "Tuition and Payment." No Date: Punahou.com. Accessed 25 June 2008.

won a scholarship Janny Scott. "A Free-Spirited Wanderer Who Set Obama's Path." 14 March 2008: NYTimes.com. Accessed 24 June 2008.

My first experience ... race Obama. *Dreams from My Father*. 58.

started fifth grade Obama. *Dreams from My Father*. 58.

black children in the class Obama. *Dreams from My Father*. 60.

p. 10   *coming for a visit* Obama. *Dreams from My Father*. 62.

For brief spells ... his company Obama. *Dreams from My Father*. 70-1

Two weeks ... gone Obama. *Dreams from My Father*. 70

p. 11   *period of destitution* Obama. *Dreams from My Father*. 323.

automobile accident Philip Ochieng. " From Home Squared to the US Senate: How Barack Obama Was Lost and Found." 1 November 2004: NationMedia.com. Accessed 24 June 2008.

Sometimes ... priority list Obama. *Dreams from My Father.* 75

with his grandparents Janny Scott. "A Free-Spirited Wanderer Who Set Obama's Path." 24 March 2008: NYTimes.com. Accessed 24 June 2008.

p. 12   *I was trying ... what that meant* Obama. *Dreams from My Father.* 76

utterly alone Obama. *Dreams from My Father.* 91.

I got high ... my mind Obama. *Dreams from My Father.* 93.

hoped for change Obama. *Dreams from My Father.* 74.

play like ... that way Obama. *Dreams from My Father.* 74. The discussion was with a composite figure Obama calls Ray. The character is based on a real person named Keith Kakugawa, who approached Obama's campaign in 2007. He had become a homeless person in Los Angeles and served prison time for a parole violation. "He wasn't this all-smiling kid," Kakugawa told ABC News. "He was a kid that would be going through adolescence, minus parents, feeling abandoned and, you know, inner turmoil with himself. He did have a lot of race issues, inner race issues, being both black and white." *Nightline,* ABC News., April 2007. Cited in Mendell. Obama. *Obama,* 41.

p. 13   *withdrawal ... your own defeat* Obama. *Dreams from My Father.* 85.

People ... sudden moves Obama. *Dreams from My Father.* 94.

had been admitted Mendell. *Obama.* 56.

p. 14   *I rose ... narrow and small* Obama. *Dreams from My Father.* 110.

You know ... natural temperament Larissa MacFarquhar. "The Conciliator: Where is Barack Obama coming from?" 7 May 2007: NewYorker.com. Accessed 23 June 2008.

p. 15   *wanted all of this* Obama. *Dreams from My Father.* 115.

vacant lot next door Shira Boss-Bicak. "Barack Obama '83: Is He the New Face of The Democratic Party?" January 2005: Columbia.edu. Accessed 25 June 2008. See Obama. Dreams from My Father. 118.

his stepfather in 1980 Amanda Ripley. "The Story of Barack Obama's Mother," 9 April 2008: Time.com.

p. 16   *into his studies* Shira Boss-Bicak. "Barack Obama '83: Is He the New Face of The Democratic Party?" January 2005: Columbia.edu. Accessed 25 June 2008

international relations Janny Scott, "Obama's Account of New York Years Often Differs From What Others Say." 20 October 2007: NYTimes.com.

nuclear disarmament Bwog.net. "Obama's Schoolwork: Verily, a Mystery." 25 July 2008: Bwog.net. Accessed 31 July 2008.

At night ... freedom songs Obama. *Dreams from My Father.* 134.

p. 17   *businesses operate overseas* The firm was later acquired by the Economist magazine's Economist Intelligence Unit. Economist Group. "Our history." 2007: EconomistGroup.com. Accessed 14 July 2008.

Business International Money Report Janny Scott. "Obama's Account of New York Years Often Differs From What Others Say." 30 October 2007: NYTimes.com.

Forget ... make you some money Obama. *Dreams from My Father.* 136.

p. 18   *trying to ... recycling* Obama. *Dreams from My Father.* 139.

mass transit ... financial aid issues Janny Scott. "Obama's Account of New York Years Often Differs From What Others Say." 30 October 2007: NYTimes.com.

In six months ... soup from a can Obama. *Dreams from My Father.* 139.

led by white priests Bob Secter and John McCormick. "Portrait of a pragmatist: As a raw community organizer in Chicago in the `80s, Obama preached reaching out to attain goals." 30 March 2007: ChicagoTribune.com. See Obama. Dreams from My Father. 150, 166.

called back Mendell. *Obama.* 71-2.

community in the country Mendell. *Obama.* 65.

allowance to buy a car Obama. *Dreams from My Father.* 142.

p. 19   *two freeways* U.S. Census, Record Information Services. Cited in Wikipedia. "Roseland, Chicago." 14 June 2008: Wikipedia.org. Accessed 26 June 2008.

Power comes ... people Eric Norden. "Interview with Saul Alinsky." 1972: *Playboy Magazine* rpt. No Date: Progress.org. Accessed 25 June 2008.

p. 20 *Once I ... build power* Obama. *Dreams from My Father.* 155

The only answer ... goals Eric Norden. "Interview with Saul Alinsky." 1972: *Playboy Magazine* rpt. No Date: Progress.org. Accessed 25 June 2008.

97 percent African American The Field Museum. "Journey Through Calumet: Riverdale (Altgeld Gardens) Boundaries and Major Infrastructure." 2007: FieldMuseum.org. Accessed 25 June 2008.

hearty applause Obama. *Dreams from My Father.* 185.

p. 21 *a fundamental way* Obama. *Dreams from My Father.* 242.

but not both Obama. *Dreams from My Father.* 247-8.

Washington ... Altgeld Mendell. *Obama.* 83.

p. 22 *I would learn ... fire* Obama. *Dreams from My Father.* 276

When I ... company of books Obama. *Dreams from My Father.* 188

made little impression Mendell. *Obama.* 72.

p. 23 *Anglo-American Puritanism* Trinity United Church of Christ. "About Us." No Date: TUCC.org. Accessed 26 June 2008.

8,500 by the 1980s Howard University. "The Biography of the Reverend Jeremiah A. Wright. No Date: Howard.edu. Accessed 26 June 2008.

Oprah Winfrey Mendell. *Obama.* 75.

It might help ... really Obama, *Dreams from My Father.* 274.

never enough Obama. *Dreams from My Father.* 279.

Probably never will be Obama. *Dreams from My Father.* 284.

By widening ... organizing Obama. *Dreams from My Father.* 286

7:30 a.m. Obama. *Dreams from My Father.* 291

The Audacity of Hope Manya A. Brachear. "Rev. Jeremiah A. Wright, Jr.: Pastor inspires Obama's 'audacity.'" 21 January 2007 : ChicagoTribune.com. Accessed 29 June 2008.

White folks' ... That's the world! Obama. *Dreams from My Father.* 293

The audacity ... find it Obama. *Dreams from My Father.* 294. The full text of a similar sermon by Jeremiah Wright titled "Audacity To Hope" delivered in 1990 was printed by *The Atlantic* in 2008. Andrew Sullivan. "For The Record." 16 Mar 2008: AndrewSullivan.TheAtlantic.com. Accessed 27 June 2008.

p. 24 *The blood ... world* Obama. *Dreams from My Father.* 294

down his cheeks Obama. *Dreams from My Father.* 295

submitted ... truth See Obama, *Audacity of Hope*, 208. See Mendell, *Obama*, 75.

Sidley & Austin in Chicago Law Review selection: Harvard Law Review. "2008 Harvard Law Review Membership Selection Policies." 21 June 2008: HarvardLawReview.org. Harvard Law enrollment: Harvard Law School. "Harvard Law School Facts." 21 June 2008: Law.Harvard.edu.

p. 25 *largest in the country* Sidley Austin. "Our Firm: History." No Date: Sidley.com. Accessed 26 June 2008.

Harvard Law in 1988 Richard Wolffe. "Barack's Rock: She's the one who keeps him real, the one who makes sure running for leader of the free world doesn't go to his head. Michelle's story." 25 February 2008: Newsweek.com. Accessed 25 June 2008.

world as it should be Richard Wolffe. "Barack's Rock: She's the one who keeps him real, the one who makes sure running for leader of the free world doesn't go to his head. Michelle's story." 25 February 2008: Newsweek.com. Accessed 25 June 2008.

racial and ethnic conflict Scott Fornek. "Michelle Obama: 'He swept me off my feet:' 15th Wedding Anniversary, Obamas recall first date, proposal that 'shut up' Michelle. 3 October 2007: SunTimes.com. Accessed 26 June 2008.

p. 26 *support to him* Michael Levenson and Jonathan Saltzman, "At Harvard Law, a unifying voice: Classmates recall Obama as even-handed leader," 28 January 2007: Boston.com. Accessed 20 June 2008.

his memoirs Fox Butterfield. "First Black Elected to Head Harvard's Law Review." 6 February 1990: NYTimes.com. See Mendell. *Obama.* 89. Accessed 20 June 2008.

If the politicians … them Gretchen Reynolds. "Vote of Confidence: A huge black turnout in November 1992 altered Chicago's electoral landscape—and raised a new political star: a 31-year-old lawyer named Barack Obama." January 1993: ChicagoMag.com. Accessed 23 June 2008.

Mayor Daley Anne E. Kornblut. "Michelle Obama's Career Timeout: For Now, Weight Shifts in Work-Family Tug of War." 11 May 2007: WashingtonPost.com. Accessed 25 June 2008.

shuts you up Scott Fornek. "Michelle Obama: 'He swept me off my feet:' 15th Wedding Anniversary, Obamas recall first date, proposal that 'shut up' Michelle. 3 October 2007: SunTimes.com. Accessed 26 June 2008.

p. 27 *Lecturer, an adjunct position* Domenico Montanaro. "Professor v. Senior Lecturer." 28 March 2008: MSNBC.MSN.com. Accessed 24 June 2008.

Davis, Miner, Barnhill & Galland Miner, Barnhill, & Galland corporate website. 2008: LawMBG.com. Accessed 23 June 2008.

Joyce Foundation board Wikipedia. "Barack Obama: Early Life and Career." 26 June 2008: Wikipedia.org. Accessed 25 June 2008.

p. 28 *Public Allies in 1993* Karen Springen. "First Lady in Waiting: Native Chicagoan Michelle Obama married a skinny kid with a funny name. She's keeping it real." October 2004: ChicagoMag.com. Accessed 25 June 2008.

She agreed David Jackson and Ray Long. "Obama knows his way around a ballot: Some say his ability to play political hardball goes back to his first campaign." 3 April 2007: ChicagoTribune.com.

first campaign for public office David Jackson and Ray Long. "Obama knows his way around a ballot: Some say his ability to play political hardball goes back to his first campaign." 3 April 2007: ChicagoTribune.com.

Hyde Park Herald cited in Ryan Lizza. "Making It: How Chicago shaped Obama." 21 July 2008: NewYorker.com. Accessed 23 July 2008.

In this room … torch Amanda Ripley. "The Story of Barack Obama's Mother," 9 April 2008: Time.com. Accessed 20 June 2008.

I owe to her Obama. *Dreams from My Father.* xii.

p. 29 *December deadline* David Jackson and Ray Long. "Obama knows his way around a ballot: Some say his ability to play political hardball goes back to his first campaign." 3 April 2007: ChicagoTribune.com.

p. 30 *What if … before them* Hank De Zutter. "What Makes Obama Run? Lawyer, teacher, philanthropist, and author Barack Obama doesn't need another career. But he's entering politics to get back to his true passion — community organization." 8 December 1995: ChicagoReader.com. Accessed 28 June 2008.

three other rivals David Jackson and Ray Long. "Obama knows his way around a ballot: Some say his ability to play political hardball goes back to his first campaign." 3 April 2007: ChicagoTribune.com.

My conclusion … going to be David Jackson and Ray Long. "Obama knows his way around a ballot: Some say his ability to play political hardball goes back to his first campaign." 3 April 2007: ChicagoTribune.com.

two-year term "That's what happens in Chicago," said Alderwoman Toni Preckwinkle, one of his supporters. Scott Helman. "Early defeat launched a rapid political climb." 12 October 2007: Boston.com. Accessed 28 June 2008.

Democratic forces in the Senate Mendell. *Obama.* 124.

political godfather Scott Helman. "Early defeat launched a rapid political climb." 12 October 2007: Boston.com. Accessed 28 June 2008.

52-4 in May 1998 Mendell. *Obama.* 124. The Washington Post said the new legislation made Illinois, "one of the best in the nation on campaign finance disclosure." Charles Peters. "Judge Him by His Laws." 4 January 2008: WashingtonPost.com. Accessed 2 July 2008.

p. 31 *property losses* Mendell. *Obama.* 126

Malia Ann Lynn Sweet. "The scoop from Washington: Sweet Iowa July 4th blog special. Obama family stumps; Malia's birthday, Oskaloosa bookstore rings up sales. Report 5." 4 July 2007: SunTimes.com. Accessed 2 July 2008.

promoted to Senior Lecturer University of Chicago Law School. "Statement Regarding Barack Obama." No Date: Chicago.edu. Accessed 30 June 2008.

reelected to the Senate Seats in the Chicago Senate alternate between two- and four-year terms. Wikipedia. "Illinois Senate." 29 June 2008: Wikipedia.org. Accessed 1 July 2008. For Obama's election see Office of Illinois State Senator Barack Obama, 13th District. State House website. No Date: Archive.org. Accessed 30 June 2008.

bipartisan majorities Mendell. *Obama*. 128-9.

p. 32 *follow Harold Washington* Mendell. *Obama*. 128.

blamed his wife Neal Pollack. "Rush to defeat: Chicago Mayor Richard Daley is a shoo-in thanks to a weak campaign by a congressman who should have been a contender." 23 February 1999: Salon.com.

stop campaigning Mendell. *Obama*. 133.

white man in blackface Ted Kleine. "Is Bobby Rush in Trouble?: Two formidable opponents in the race for his congressional seat are banking on it." 17 March 2000: ChicagoReader.com.

p. 33 *trip to Hawaii over public safety* Mendell. *Obama*. 136.

We called him ... March 2000 primary Scott Helman. "Early defeat launched a rapid political climb." 12 October 2007: Boston.com. Accessed 28 June 2008.

left disheartened Mendell. *Obama*. 144

The notion ... seemed pretty thin Mendell. *Obama*. 150.

Natasha "Sasha" Obama Kathy Kiely. "Obama reaching out to white working class." 6 June 2008: USAToday.com. Accessed 2 July 2008.

state-wide redistricting Michael C. Herron and Alan E. Wiseman. "Gerrymanders and Theories of Law Making: A Study of Legislative Redistricting in Illinois." The Journal of Politics 70.1. January 2008: Journals.Cambridge.org. Accessed 24 July 2008.

Obama's district Ryan Lizza. "Making It: How Chicago shaped Obama." 21 July 2008: NewYorker.com. Accessed 23 July 2008.

p. 34 *meeting with Penny Pritzker* Mendell. *Obama*. 154-6. A few months later, reporter Mendell wrote, "it seemed that every member of the Pritzker clan had given the new maximum of twelve thousand dollars to Obama." Mendell. *Obama*. 210.

David Axelrod Robert G. Kaiser. "The Player at Bat: David Axelrod, the Man With Obama's Game Plan, Is Also the Candidate's No. 1 Fan." 2 May 2008: WashingtonPost.com. Accessed 30 June 2008. See Scott Helman. "Early defeat launched a rapid political climb." 12 October 2007: Boston.com. Accessed 28 June 2008.

p. 35 *I don't oppose all wars ... income* Barack Obama. "Remarks of Illinois State Sen. Barack Obama Against Going to War with Iraq." 2 October 2002: BarackObama.com. Accessed 30 June 2008.

most proud of Mendell. *Obama*. 176.

You can make the next U.S. senator Mendell. *Obama*. 180.

Chair of Health and Human Services Jackie Calmes. "Statehouse Yields Clues to Obama." 23 February 2007: WSJ.com. Accessed 26 June 2008.

p. 36 *legislative track record* New York Times. "Obama's Record in Illinois Senate." 29 July 2007: NYTimes.com. Accessed 30 June 2008. Taping requirement: Monica Davey. "Illinois Will Require Taping Of Homicide Interrogations." 17 July 2003: NYTimes.com. "You got somebody good," Jones said later, "you push him." Scott Helman. "Early defeat launched a rapid political climb." 12 October 2007: Boston.com. Accessed 28 June 2008.

Obama announced his candidacy "I think that, plainly, one of the lessons he learned from 2000 was start early, plan well, do the hard work of laying a foundation," Axelrod said. Scott Helman. "Early defeat launched a rapid political climb." 12 October 2007: Boston.com. Accessed 28 June 2008.

Blair Hull Monica Davey. "Closely Watched Illinois Senate Race Attracts 7 Candidates in Millionaire Range." 7 March 2004: NYTimes.com. Accessed 28 June 2008. A potentially devastating competitor was eliminated when Carol Mosely Braun, Fitzgerald's predecessor and the first African American woman in history to be elected to the U.S. Senate, announced after weeks of indecision that she would run for President.

Dan Hynes Mendell. *Obama.* 182.

$40 million to win the race Monica Davey. "Closely Watched Illinois Senate Race Attracts 7 Candidates in Millionaire Range." 7 March 2004: NYTimes.com. Accessed 28 June 2008.

p. 37   *arrested for allegedly hitting her* Mendell. *Obama.* 215.

"Yes, we can" slogan Mendell. *Obama.* 229.

won the Democratic primary David Mendell. "Obama routs Democratic foes; Ryan tops crowded GOP field." 17 March 2004: ChicagoTribune.com. Accessed 26 June 2008.

I'm really going to miss those little girls Mendell. *Obama.* 243.

Jack Ryan Monica Davey. "Closely Watched Illinois Senate Race Attracts 7 Candidates in Millionaire Range." 7 March 2004: NYTimes.com. Accessed 28 June 2008.

George Soros ... Hillary Clinton Mendell. *Obama.* 248.

p. 38   *sex clubs in New York and Paris* "It was a bizarre club with cages, whips and other apparatus hanging from the ceiling," Jeri Ryan said of the New York club in the court filings. Her husband, she added, "wanted me to have sex with him there, with another couple watching. I refused." When she arrived at the club in Paris, she said, "people were having sex everywhere. I cried. I was physically ill. [He] became very upset with me and said it was not a 'turn on' for me to cry." CNN. "Ex-wife of GOP Senate candidate alleged sex club forays." 22 June 2004: CNN.com. Accessed 30 June 2008.

Ryan withdrew CNN. "Ryan drops out of Senate race in Illinois: Campaign hurt by sex club allegations." 25 June 2004: CNN.com. Accessed 25 June 2008.

p. 40   *Hope ... better days ahead* Barack Obama. "Keynote Address at the 2004 Democratic National Convention." 27 July 2004: BarackObama.com. Accessed 23 June 2008.

Alan Keyes nominated Juliet Eilperin. "Keyes to Face Obama in U.S. Senate Race." 9 August 2004: WashingtonPost.com. Accessed 25 June 2008.

Alan Keyes background Obama. *The Audacity of Hope.* 212.

Obama victory Associated Press. "Obama wins Senate race to become 5th black U.S. senator in history." 2 November 2004: USAToday.com. Accessed 30 June 2008.

p. 41   *sworn in ... Dick Cheney* Office of Senator Barack Obama. "About Barack Obama: United States Senator for Illinois." No Date: Senate.gov. Accessed 30 June 2008.

p. 42   *iron can't get any hotter* Ryan Lizza. "Making It: How Chicago shaped Obama." 21 July 2008: NewYorker.com. Accessed 23 July 2008.

He quit smoking Mendell. *Obama.* 380.

Each and every time ... a new birth of freedom on this Earth Barack Obama. "Full Text of Senator Barack Obama's Announcement for President Springfield, IL." 10 February 2007: BarackObama.com. Accessed 29 June 2008.

p. 43   *tools at My.BarackObama.com* Obama for America. "The Blueprint for Change: Barack Obama's Plan for America." 20 February 2007: BarackObama.com. Accessed 2 July 2008.

p. 44   *We will do ... privately* Obama. *The Audacity of Hope.* 159.

at the heart ... since its founding Obama. *The Audacity of Hope.* 149.

resources vibrant free market Obama. *The Audacity of Hope.* 152.

platform New York Times. "The Issues: Economy/Taxes." 2 July 2008: NYTimes.com Accessed 2 July 2008. See Obama for America. "The Blueprint for Change: Barack Obama's Plan for America." 20 February 2007: BarackObama.com. Accessed 2 July 2008.11-15.

p. 45   *should never ... been waged* Barack Obama. "Obama Statement on Senate Debate Over Redeploying U.S. Troops from Iraq." 18 July 2007: Obama.Senate.gov. Accessed 17 July 2008.

not maintain permanent bases New York Times. "The Issues: Iraq." 2 July 2008: NY-Times.com Accessed 2 July 2008. On permanent bases see Obama for America. "The Blueprint for Change: Barack Obama's Plan for America." 20 February 2007: BarackObama.com. Accessed 17 July 2008. 51.

residual force Obama for America. "The Blueprint for Change: Barack Obama's Plan for America." 20 February 2007: BarackObama.com. 51. Accessed 17 July 2008.

safe havens in Pakistan Obama for America. "The Blueprint for Change: Barack Obama's Plan for America." 20 February 2007: BarackObama.com. 54. Accessed 17 July 2008.

p.46   *military force* New York Times. "The Issues: Iraq." 2 July 2008: NYTimes.com Accessed 2 July 2008.

Guantanamo Bay Obama for America. "The Blueprint for Change: Barack Obama's Plan for America." 20 February 2007: BarackObama.com. 50-1. Accessed 17 July 2008.

control its future Obama. *The Audacity of Hope*. 171.

Obama for America. "The Blueprint for Change: Barack Obama's Plan for America." 20 February 2007: BarackObama.com. 24-7. Accessed 17 July 2008.

sustainable sources by 2025 New York Times. "The Issues: Climate Change." 2 July 2008: NYTimes.com Accessed 2 July 2008.

In a world … bargain Obama. *The Audacity of Hope*. 159.

highest dropout rates Obama for America. "The Blueprint for Change: Barack Obama's Plan for America." 20 February 2007: BarackObama.com. 21. Accessed 17 July 2008.

education proposals Obama for America. "The Blueprint for Change: Barack Obama's Plan for America." 20 February 2007: BarackObama.com. 25-8. Accessed 17 July 2008.

p. 47 *health care proposals* Obama for America. "The Blueprint for Change: Barack Obama's Plan for America." 20 February 2007: BarackObama.com. 6-9. Accessed 2 July 2008. See Obama. The Audacity of Hope. 184-5.

lagged far behind Pollster.com. "2008 National Democratic Presidential Primary." 3 June 2008: Pollster.com. Accessed 3 July 2008.

p. 48 *campaign website* Obama for America. 2 July 2008: My.BarackObama.com. Accessed 2 July 2008.

Facebook Brian Beutler. "Obama Facebook group rockets toward one-million." 26 January 2007: RawStory.com. Accessed 1 July 2008.

biggest pro-Clinton group Seth Gitell. "Obama's Facebook." 13 February 2007: NYSun.com. Accessed 2 July 2008.

Obama application Kashay Sanders. "Facebook co-founder pulls for Obama." 15 November 2007: TheDartmouth.org. Accessed 1 July 2008.

31 March fundraising Washington Post. "Campaign Finance: First Quarter 2007 FEC Filings" 31 March 2007: WashingtonPost.com. Accessed 1 July 2008.

p. 49 *average size of Obama donations* A Rasmussen poll released on 22 January found Clinton with 31 percent, Obama with 24 percent and Edwards with 12 percent, and the other candidates far behind. Rasmussen. "Weekly Presidential Tracking Polling History." 22 January 2008: RasmussenReports.com. Accessed 1 July 2008.

refused money from lobbyists Jonathan D. Salant. "Clinton Gets Most Lobbyist Money, McCain Most Help (Update1)." 4 February 2008: Bloomberg.com. Accessed 3 July 2008.

criss-crossed the country New York Times. "Candidate Schedules." 2 July 2008: NYTimes.com. Accessed 2 July 2008.

Obama Girl Jake Tapper. "Music Video Has a 'Crush on Obama'." 13 June 2007: ABCNews.go.com. Accessed 27 June 2008. The video had been seen 8.8 million times by July 2008. Obama Girl. "I Got a Crush. . .On Obama." 13 June 2007: YouTube.com. Accessed 2 July 2008.

2 July fundraising Jim Malone. "Obama Fundraising Suggests Close Race for Party Nominations." Voice of America. 2 July 2007: VoANews.com. Accessed 27 June 2008.

Oprah Winfrey endorsement Jeff Zeleny. "Oprah Winfrey Hits Campaign Trail for Obama." 9 December 2007: NYTimes.com. Accessed 27 June 2008.

p. 50 *94.6 percent white* U.S. Census Bureau. "State & County QuickFacts." 2 January 2008: Census.gov. Accessed 1 July 2008.

Iowa results CNN. "Iowa caucus turnout shatters record." 3 January 2008: CNN.com. Accessed 2 July 2008. For 2004 turnout: Michael McDonald. "2004 Presidential Primary Turnout Rates." 23 February 2008: GMU.edu. Accessed 1 July 2008. "37 field offices." Evan Thomas. "Chapter 2: Back From the Dead." In "Secrets of the 2008 Campaign." 5 November 2008: Newsweek.com. Accessed 15 November 2008.

p. 51 *On this January night ... hope* Barack Obama. "Remarks of Senator Barack Obama: Iowa Caucus Night." 3 January 2008: BarackObama.com. Accessed 1 July 2008.

false hopes ABC News. "Transcript: ABC News/Facebook/WMUR Democratic Debate, Four Democratic Contenders Debate in New Hampshire." 5 January 2008: ABCNews.go.com. Accessed 1 July 2008.

choked up CNN. "Clinton chokes up, is applauded, at campaign stop." 7 January 2008: CNN.com. Accessed 1 July 2008.

p. 52 *New Hampshire results* New York Times. "Primary Season Election Results." 3 June 2008: NYTimes.com. Accessed 1 July 2008.

take a while Evan Thomas. "Chapter 1: How He Did It." In "Secrets of the 2008 Campaign." 5 November 2008: Newsweek.com. Accessed 15 November 2008.

Michigan results New York Times. "Primary Season Election Results." 3 June 2008: NYTimes.com. Accessed 1 July 2008.

Nevada results New York Times. "Primary Season Election Results." 3 June 2008: NYTimes.com. Accessed 1 July 2008.

p. 53 *Kucinich dropped out* Mark Naymik and Molly Kavanoaugh. "Kucinich drops presidential bid." 24 January 2008: Cleveland.com. Accessed 1 July 2008.

Obama on South Carolina Conferate flag: Barack Obama. "A More Perfect Union." 18 March 2008: BarackObama.com. Accessed 1 July 2008. U.S. Census Bureau. State & County QuickFacts. 2 January 2008: Census.gov. Accessed 1 July 2008.

South Carolina results CNN. "Exit Polls: South Carolina." 26 January 2008: CNN.com. Accessed 1 July 2008.

campaign organizations Matt Stoller. "Some Campaign Observations." 26 January 2008: OpenLeft.org. Accessed 1 July 2008.

Bill Clinton comment on South Carolina Jake Tapper. "Bubba: Obama Is Just Like Jesse Jackson." 26 January 2008: ABCNews.com. Accessed 1 July 2008.

Kennedy endorsement Associated Press. "Kennedys endorse Obama." 28 January 2008: MSN.com. Accessed 1 July 2008.

MoveOn.org endorsement MoveOn.org. "MoveOn Endorsement Throws Progressive Weight Behind Barack Obama. 3.2 Million Members Nationwide Mobilize to Get Out the Progressive Vote for Senator Obama: Group Has Over 1.7 Million Members In Super Tuesday States." 1 February 2008: MoveOn.org. Accessed 1 July 2008.

p. 54 *Florida results* New York Times. "Primary Season Election Results." 3 June 2008: NYTimes.com. Accessed 1 July 2008.

Edwards dropped out Julie Bosman and Jeff Zeleny. "Edwards Drops Out of Democratic Race." 30 January 2008: NYTimes.com. Accessed 2 July 2008.

delegates for nomination The number of delegates needed for nomination changed over the course of the campaign because of the disputed status of primary elections in Florida and Michigan. In the end, 2,117.5 delegates were required for nomination. CNN. "Election Center 2008." 2 July 2008: CNN.com. Accessed 4 July 2008.

Super Tuesday results New York Times. "Primary Season Election Results." 3 June 2008: NYTimes.com. Accessed 1 July 2008.

Clinton $5 million loan Kate Snow and Teddy Davis. "Clinton Loaned Campaign $5 Million." 6 February 2008: ABCNews.com. Accessed 4 July 2008.

p. 56 *plagiarism allegation* Jeff Zeleny. "An Obama Refrain Bears Echoes of a Governor's Speeches." 18 February 2008: NYTimes.com. Accessed 1 July 2008.

traditional Somali dress Celeste Katz and Michael Saul. "Dust up over Somali photo has Barack Obama and Hillary Clinton fighting hard." 26 February 2008: DailyNews.com. Accessed 4 July 2008.

Senator Dodd endorsement Michael Powell and John Sullivan. "Dodd Endorses Obama for President." 26 February 2008: NYTimes.com. Accessed 2 July 2008.

only a matter of time "No matter how you cut it, Obama will almost certainly end the primaries with a pledged-delegate lead, courtesy of all those landslides in February," Jonathan Alter wrote in Newsweek on 4 March. Jonathan Alter. "Hillary's Math Problem: Forget tonight. She could win 16 straight and still lose." 4 March 2008: Newsweek.com. Accessed 2 July 2008. Stories of infighting in the Clinton campaign begin to appear. Peter Nicholas. No Title. Los Angeles Times. 3 May: LATimes.com. Accessed 3 July 2008. See Peter Baker and Jim Rutenberg. "The Long Road to a Clinton Exit: After a cascading series of defeats in February, Hillary Rodham Clinton's three-month effort to salvage her campaign failed." 8 June 2008: NYTimes.com. Accessed 2 July 2008.

John McCain clinched Michelle R. Smith. "Clinton wins Rhode Island; McCain secures nomination." March 5, 2008: Boston.com. Accessed 27 June 2008.

p. 57   *Davis joins Rezko partnership* Tim Novak. "Obama's letters for Rezko, Not a Favor? As a state senator, he went to bat for now-indicted developer's deal." 13 June 2007: SunTimes.com. Accessed 3 July 2008.

help people in his district Tim Novak. "Obama's letters for Rezko, Not a Favor? As a state senator, he went to bat for now-indicted developer's deal." 13 June 2007: SunTimes.com. Accessed 3 July 2008.

Rezko connections Chris Fusco, David McKinney, Tim Novak and Abdon M. Pallasch. "Obama explains Rezko relationship to Sun-Times." 16 March 2008: SunTimes.com. Accessed 4 July 2008.

totaled about $250,000 Chris Fusco, David McKinney, Tim Novak and Abdon M. Pallasch. "Obama explains Rezko relationship to Sun-Times." 16 March 2008: SunTimes.com. Accessed 4 July 2008. See Sarah Wheaton. "Obama Elaborates on Rezko Relationship." 14 March 2008: NYTimes.com. Accessed 3 July 2008.

p. 58   *best price he could get* Timothy J. Burger. "Obama Bought Home Without Rezko Discount, Seller Says (Update1)." 18 February 2008: Bloomberg.com. Accessed 3 July 2008.

bought one-sixth of the lot Dave McKinney and Chris Fusco. "Obama on Rezko deal: It was a mistake." 5 November 2006: SunTimes.com. Accessed 23 June 2008.

boneheaded mistake Tim Novak. "Obama's letters for Rezko, Not a Favor? As a state senator, he went to bat for now-indicted developer's deal." 13 June 2007: SunTimes.com. Accessed 3 July 2008.

give donations to charity Just one person linked to Rezko, financier and Hollywood producer Thomas Rosenberg, contributed to Obama's Presidential campaign. Kenneth P. Vogel. "Obama releases names of Rezko-linked donors." 17 March 2008: Politico.com. Accessed 3 July 2008.

convicted on 16 counts Bob Secter and Jeff Coen. "Rezko convicted of corruption." 4 June 2008: ChicagoTribune.com. Accessed 2 July 2008. He went to prison immediately. WLS-TV. "Political fundraiser found guilty on 16 counts: Rezko begins serving time immediately." 5 June 2008: ABC.Go.com. Accessed 2 July 2008.

p. 59   *chickens home to roost* Brian Ross and Rehab El-Buri. "Obama's Pastor:God Damn America." 13 March 2008: ABCNews.com. Accessed 27 June 2008.

said he was not present Barack Obama. "On My Faith and My Church." 14 March 2008: HuffingtonPost.com. Accessed 3 July 2008.

p. 60   *choice ... not this time* Barack Obama. "A More Perfect Union" 18 March 2008: BarackObama.com. Accessed 1 July 2008.

p. 61   *Bittergate* Allison Keyes. "Obama Catches Flak for Remarks on Working Class." NPR. April 12, 2008: NPR.org. Accessed 27 June 2008.

16 April ABC News debate New York Times. "Transcript: Democratic Debate in Philadelphia." 16 April 2008: NYTimes.com. Accessed 3 July 2008.

valued member of the … community Mike Dorning and Rick Pearson. "Daley: Don't tar Obama for Ayers." 17 April 2008: TRB.com. Accessed 3 July 2008.

bombing public buildings Brent Staples. "The Oldest Rad." 30 September 2001: NYTimes.com. Accessed 27 June 2008.

p. 62 *organized an event* Joanna Weiss. "How Obama and the radical became news: Story highlights the path from blog to mainstream." 18 April 2008: Boston.com. Accessed 2 July 2008.

notion … doesn't make much sense New York Times. "Transcript: Democratic Debate in Philadelphia." 16 April 2008: NYTimes.com. Accessed 3 July 2008.

game … smarter than that New York Times. "Transcript: Democratic Debate in Philadelphia." 16 April 2008: NYTimes.com. Accessed 3 July 2008.

Clinton needed Jonathan Alter. "Hillary's New Math Problem: Tuesday's big wins? The delegate calculus just got worse." 5 March 2008: Newsweek.com. Accessed 3 July 2008.

Pennsylvania results New York Times. "Primary Season Election Results." 3 June 2008: NYTimes.com. Accessed 1 July 2008.

Rev. Wright on AIDS and 9/11 Rev. Jeremiah Wright. "Transcript: Speech to National Press Club." 28 April 2008: ChicagoTribune.com. Accessed 1 July 2008.

bunch of rants Kathy Kiely and David Jackson. "Obama breaks with former pastor. Candidate cites rants on U.S. role in terror, AIDS." 29 April 2008: USAToday.com. Accessed 2 July 2008.

p. 63 *declined to concede* Mark Silva. "Obama defeats Clinton in North Carolina." 6 May 2008: ChicagoTribune.com. Accessed 1 July 2008.

black man stealing my show Scott Helman. "Obama tagged with comments of another cleric: Priest mocked Clinton display of emotions." 31 May 2008: Boston.com. Accessed 2 July 2008.

answer for everything CNN. "Obama quits church, citing controversies." 31 May 2008: CNN.com. Accessed 2 July 2008.

p. 64 *more delegates than Clinton* CNN. "Florida, Michigan get all delegates, but each gets half vote." 1 June 2008: CNN.com. Accessed 3 July 2008. See Jesse Stanchak. "The New Math." 1 June 2008: Slate.com. Accessed 3 July 2008.

be the Democratic nominee CNN. "Obama: I will be the Democratic nominee." 4 June 2008: CNN.com. Accessed 3 July 2008.

stop taking money from lobbyists Nedra Pickler and Jim Kuhnhenn. "Obama keeps Dean at DNC, bans lobbyist money." 5 June 2008: News.Yahoo.com. Accessed 2 July 2008

for Barack Obama CNN. "Clinton endorses Obama, calls for party unity." 7 June 2008: CNN.com. Accessed 3 July 2008.

Unity, NH rally CNN. "Obama, Clinton to promote unity in Unity." 27 June 2008: CNN.com. Accessed 27 June 2008.

p. 65 *raised over $295 million* Federal Election Commission. "FEC Candidate Summary Reports." 2 July 2008: SDRDC.com Accessed 2 July 2008.

public financing … is broken Jonathan D. Salant, "Obama Won't Accept Public Money in Election Campaign." 19 June 2008: Bloomberg.com. Accessed 27 June 2008.

decline public funds Jonathan D. Salant, "Obama Won't Accept Public Money in Election Campaign." 19 June 2008: Bloomberg.com. Accessed 27 June 2008.

influence of special interests Obama. *The Audacity of Hope*. 134.

would be publicly funded Adam Aigner-Treworgy and Mark Murray. "McCain to accept public financing." 19 June 2008: Firstread.MSNBC.MSN.com. Accessed 19 November 2008.

p. 66 *let's go win the election* Barack Obama. "Speech to Campaign Staff and Volunteers." Early June 2008: BarackObama.com. Accessed 2 July 2008.

p. 68 *led national polls* Pollster.com. "2008 National Presidential General Election: McCain vs Obama." 5 November 2008: Pollster.com. Accessed 14 November 2008.

FightTheSmears.com Sam Graham-Felsen. "Take Action and Fight the Smears." 12 June 2008: My.BarackObama.com. Accessed 19 November 2008.

Obama Organizing Fellows Peter Slevin. "Obama Campaign Dispatching Thousands." 13 June 2008: WashingtonPost.com. Accessed 19 November 2008.

June fundraising Suzanne Goldenberg. "McCain eclipsed as TV anchors follow Obama's foreign trip." 18 July 2008: Guardian.co.uk. Accessed 19 November 2008. Third party candidates, who played significant roles in the 2000 and 1992 presidential contests among others, attracted little support. The nominees included Independent Ralph Nader, Libertarian Bob Barr, Green Cynthia McKinney, Chuck Baldwin for the Constitution Party, defeated Republican nominee Ron Paul for the Louisiana Taxpayers Party and, remarkably, Alan Keyes for America's Independent Party, gained little support. Nader: David Ryan Palmer. "Get to know the third parties on the ballot." 3 November 2008: MorningSun.net. Accessed 15 November 2008. Barr: Raffi Khatchadourian. "The Third Man: Bob Barr's Libertarian run for the White House." 27 October 2008: NewYorker.com. Accessed 15 November 2008. McKinney: David Ryan Palmer. "Get to know the third parties on the ballot." 3 November 2008: MorningSun.net. Accessed 15 November 2008. Baldwin: Steve Kraske. 26 April 2008: KCStar.com. Accessed 15 November. Paul: David Ryan Palmer. "Get to know the third parties on the ballot." 3 November 2008: MorningSun.net. Accessed 15 November 2008. Keyes: "The 2008 Election: A Winnowing Season." 3 November 2008: AlanKeyes.com. Accessed 15 November 2008.

knew enough about world affairs David Espo. "Obama's Europe, Middle East Trip Marks First High-Profile Step Onto World Stage." Associated Press. 18 July 2008: HuffingtonPost.com. Accessed 19 November 2008.

p. 69 *media accompanied the frontrunner* Itinerary: Sunlen Miller. "Obama Plays Down Significance of Foreign Trip." 27 July 2008: ABCNews.com. Accessed 19 November 2008. Talea Miller. "Obama Trip Attracting Media Circus, Criticism from McCain Camp." 18 July 2008: PBS.org. Accessed 19 November 2008.

This is our time HuffingtonPost.com. "Obama Berlin Speech: See Video, Photos, Full Speech Transcript." 24 July 2008: HuffingtonPost.com. Accessed 19 November 2008.

the real Obama JohnMcCain.com. "Celeb." 30 July 2008: YouTube.com. Accessed 19 November 2008.

"Celebrity" ad Broadcast states: Alexander Mooney. "McCain ad compares Obama to Britney Spears, Paris Hilton." 30 July 2008: CNN.com. Accessed 19 November 2008. Transcript: Joe Miller. "Obama's Celebrity Cred: A new McCain ad calls Obama a celebrity (true) who says he'll raise taxes on electricity (false)." 30 July 2008: FactCheck.org. Accessed 19 November 2008.

Russian incursion into Georgia Elisabeth Bumiller and Michael Falcone. "Candidates' Reactions to Georgia Conflict Offer Hints at Style on Foreign Affairs." 9 August 2008: NYTimes.com. Accessed 1 December 2008.

within two or three percentage points Pollster.com. "2008 National Democratic Presidential Primary." 3 June 2008: Pollster.com. Accessed 3 July 2008. Accessed 19 November 2008.

p. 70 *network newscaster opinions* James Rainey. "In study, evidence of liberal-bias bias. Cable talking heads accuse broadcast networks of liberal bias — but a think tank finds that ABC, NBC and CBS were tougher on Barack Obama than on John McCain in recent weeks." 27 July 2008: LATimes.com. Accessed 19 November 2008.

wrinkly, white-haired guy David Saltonstall. "Paris Hilton's new attack ad fires back at 'world's oldest celebrity'—McCain." 6 August 2008: NYDailyNews.com. Video: 5 August 2008: FunnyOrDie.com. Accessed 17 November 2008.

jumped to number one Jerome Corsi. *The Obama Nation.* 1 August 2008: Amazon.com. Accessed 20 November 2008. Bestseller: Jim Rutenberg and Julie Bosman. "Book Attacking Obama Hopes to Repeat '04 Anti-Kerry Feat." 12 August 2008: NYTimes.com. Accessed 19 November 2008.

debuted at number five David Freddoso. *The Case Against Barack Obama.* 4 August 2008: Amazon.com. Accessed 19 November 2008.

bulk purchases The New York Times. "Hardcover Nonfiction" 24 August 2008: NYTImes.com. Accessed 19 November 2008.

charges by Freddoso David Freddoso. *The Case Against Barack Obama.* 2008: Regnery. *De facto* infanticide claim: Jess Henig. "Obama and 'Infanticide:' The facts about Obama's votes against 'Born Alive' bills in Illinois." 25 August 2008: FactCheck.org. Accessed 18 November 2008.

p. 71 *cut from the same cloth* Christopher Wills, Associated Press. "Two books, two styles, one target: Obama." 15 August 2008: Boston.com. Accessed 18 November 2008.

Unfit for Publication Obama for America. *Unfit for Publication*: 15 August 2008: FightTheSmears.com. Accessed 18 November 2008.

Traditional media was interested Google News. "The Obama Nation." 15 October 2008: Google.com. Accessed 18 November 2008. Google News. "Unfit for Command." 19 November 2008: Google.com. Accessed 19 November 2008.

Blogs were obsessed Google Blog Search. "The Obama Nation" 19 November 2008: Google.com. Accessed 18 November 2008. "Unfit for Command." 15 October 2008: Google.com. Accessed 19 November 2008.

cut to about three percent nationwide Pollster.com. "2008 National Presidential General Election: McCain vs Obama." 5 November 2008: Pollster.com. Accessed 14 November 2008.

Obama on Biden MSNBC. "Obama chooses Biden as running mate: Foreign Relations Committee chairman has globe-trotting credentials." 25 August 2008: MSNBC.MSN.com. Accessed 24 November 2008.

p. 73 *not ready to be President* Adam Nahourney and Jeff Zeleny. "Obama Chooses Biden as Running Mate." 23 August 2008: NYTimes.com. Accessed 18 November 2008.

Michelle Obama speech Cameron Brown, Gabriel Dance, Jonathan Ellis, Ben Gerst, Tom Jackson, Magdalena Sharpe, and Sarah Wheaton. "Transcript: Michelle Obama's 'One Nation.'" 25 August 2008: NYTimes.com. Accessed 18 November 2008. Video see: "Michelle Obama's Speech at the Democratic National Convention." 25 August 2008: NYTimes.com. Accessed 18 November 2008.

Senator Clinton speech Hillary Rodham Clinton. "Remarks as Prepared for Delivery." 26 August 2008: DemConvention.com. Accessed 18 November 2008. Video see: Cameron Brown, Gabriel Dance, Jonathan Ellis, Ben Gerst, Tom Jackson, Magdalena Sharpe, and Sarah Wheaton "Hillary Rodham Clinton's Speech at the Democratic National Convention." 26 August 2008: NYTimes.com. Accessed 18 November 2008.

p. 74 *Bill Clinton speech* Bill Clinton. "Bill Clinton." 27 August 2008: DemConvention.com. Accessed 18 November 2008. Video: Cameron Brown, Gabriel Dance, Jonathan Ellis, Ben Gerst, Tom Jackson, Magdalena Sharpe, and Sarah Wheaton. "Bill Clinton's Speech at the Democratic National Convention." 26 August 2008: NYTimes.com. Accessed 18 November 2008.

Mile High Stadium acceptance Many attendees waited much of the day to clear security checkpoints in lines that snaked for miles along elevated highways around the stadium. The stage set, a portico of Grecian columns reminiscent of an arcade at the White House, was toned down several times in response to accusations of hubris made in the "Celebrity" advertisement and associated criticisms. The night before the event, chief strategist David Axelrod ordered the lights dimmed and additional flags set behind the podium to subdue the scene further. Evan Thomas. "Chapter 5. Center Stage: Obama's aides worried the Clintons might steal the show. McCain revved up his campaign with an impulsive choice—Sarah Palin." In "Secrets of the 2008 Campaign." 5 November 2008: Newsweek.com. Accessed 15 November 2008. Nonetheless, the McCain campaign derided the stage set as a "Barack-opolis," and reporters picked up on the criticism. Kate Linthicum. "John McCain derides Barack Obama's" 28 August 2008: LATimes.com. Accessed 18 November 2008.

Obama Acceptance Speech Barack Obama. "Barack Obama, Illinois." 28 August 2008: DemConvention.com. Accessed 18 November 2008. Video: Cameron Brown, Gabriel Dance, Jonathan Ellis, Ben Gerst, Tom Jackson, Magdalena Sharpe, and Sarah Wheaton. "Bill Clinton's Speech at the Democratic National Convention." 26 August 2008: NYTimes.com. Accessed 18 November 2008.

p. 76 *McCain announces Palin as running mate* Michael Cooper and Elisabeth Bumiller. "Alaskan Is McCain's Choice; First Woman on G.O.P. Ticket." 29 August 2008: NYTimes.com. Accessed 18 November 2008.

Audience for Palin's speech Nielsen Wire. "Palin Triggers RNC Ratings Spike." 4 September 2008: 4 September 2008: Nielsen.com. Accessed 18 November 2008.

Palin's acceptance speech CQ Transcriptions. "Palin's Speech at the Republican National Convention." 3 September 2008: NYTimes.com. Accessed 19 November 2008. Video: Huffington Post. "Sarah Palin RNC Convention Speech." 3 September 2008: HuffingtonPost.com. Accessed 19 November 2008. Gravina Island bridge: Wikipedia. "Gravina Island Bridge." 17 November 2008: Wikipedia.org. Accessed 19 November 2008.

p. 77   *McCain will be known as John McBrilliant* Andrew Malcolm. "Holy Limbaugh! Sarah Palin turns Rush to mush over the McCain ticket." 4 September 2008: LATimes.com. Accessed 19 November 2008.

McCain acceptance speech Cameron Brown, Gabriel Dance, Jonathan Ellis, Ben Gerst, Tom Jackson, Magdalena Sharpe, and Sarah Wheaton. " John McCain's Speech at the Republican National Convention." 4 September 2008: NYTimes.com. September 4, 2008. Accessed 19 November 2008. Video: NYTimes.com. Accessed 19 November 2008.

Enthusiasm for McCain jumped Pollster.com. "2008 National Presidential General Election: McCain vs Obama." 5 November 2008: Pollster.com. Accessed 14 November 2008.

Fannie Mae and Freddie Mac collapse Ken Sweet. Government Seizes Fannie Mae, Freddie Mac. Sunday September 7: FoxBusiness.com. Accessed 14 November 2008.

p. 78   *Lehman Brothers bankrupt* Sam Mamudi. "Lehman folds with record $613 billion debt." 15 September 2008: MarketWatch.com. Accessed 24 November 2008.

Poland GDP Wikipedia. "List of countries by GDP (PPP)" 17 November 2008: Wikipedia.org. Accessed 24 November 2008.

Merrill Lynch acquired Andrew Ross Sorkin. "Lehman Files for Bankruptcy; Merrill Is Sold." 14 September 2008: NYTimes.com. Accessed 14 November 2008.

fundamentals of our economy are strong HuffingtonPost.com. "McCain On 'Black Monday': Fundamentals Of Our Economy Are Still Strong." 15 September 2008: HuffingtonPost.com. Accessed 15 November 2008.

what economy are you talking about ... meant American workers Evan Thomas. "Secrets of the 2008 Campaign. Center Stage: Obama's aides worried the Clintons might steal the show. McCain revved up his campaign with an impulsive choice—Sarah Palin." 6 November 2008. Newsweek.com. Accessed 15 November 2008.

p. 79   *Paulson proposal* FoxNews.com "McCain Suspends Campaign to Help With Bailout." 24 September 2008: FoxNews.com. Accessed 15 November 2008. Paulson plan: Department of the Treasury. "Text of Draft Proposal for Bailout Plan." 20 September 2008: NYTimes.com. Accessed 15 November 2008.

more than one thing at once CNN. "McCain, Obama headed to Washington for bailout talks." 25 September 2008: CNN.com. Accessed 15 November 2008.

Washington Mutual Savings Bank collapsed Eric Dash and Andrew Ross Sorkin. "Government Seizes WaMu and Sells Some Assets." 25 September 2008: NYTimes.com. Accessed 1 December 2008.

broke up in acrimony Fox News. "Bailout Talks Disintegrate Into Verbal Brawl; Fate Uncertain." 26 September 2008: FoxNews.com. Accessed 15 November 2008.

p. 80   *Freddie Mac paid Rick Davis* Jackie Calmes and David D. Kirkpatrick. "McCain Aide's Firm Was Paid by Freddie Mac." 23 September 2008: NYTimes.com. See Keith Epstein. "A Federal Probe of Fannie and Freddie: The mortgage giants have received grand-jury subpoenas on accounting and governance matters as the FBI widens its financial probe." 30 September 2008: BusinessWeek.com. Accessed 15 November 2008.

putting something in his Metamucil Huffington Post. "John McCain Cancels Letterman Appearance, Keith Olbermann Fills In." 24 September 2008: HuffingtonPost.com. Accessed 15 November 2008.

p. 81   *Obama and McCain debate* CQ Transcriptions. The First Presidential Debate. 26 September 2008: NYTimes.com. Accessed 15 November 2008.

p. 82   *Obama the winner* Rebecca Sinderbrand. "Round 1 in debates goes to Obama, poll says." 27 September 2008: CNN.com. Accessed 15 November 2008.

House rejected Paulson's plan U.S. House. "Final Vote Results for Roll Call 674." 29 September 2008: House.gov. Accessed 15 November 2008.

worst single-day drop in two decades Vikas Bajaj and Michael M. Grynbaum. "For Stocks, Worst Single-Day Drop in Two Decades." 29 September 2008: NYTimes.com. Accessed 15 November 2008.

in lock step Paulson's plan finally was approved on 3 October after the addition of about $150 billion in tax credits and deductions to woo holdout legislators. David M. Herszenhorn. "Bailout Plan Wins Approval; Democrats Vow Tighter Rules." 3 October 2008: NYTimes.com. Accessed 15 November 2008.

jet didn't sell Anne E. Kornblut. "Plane Not Sold on eBay." 1 September 2008: WashingtonPost.com. Accessed 15 November 2008.

p. 83   *Bridge to Nowhere* Yereth Rosen. "Palin 'bridge to nowhere' line angers many Alaskans." 1 September 2008: Reuters.com. Accessed 15 November 2008.

Bush Doctrine Charlie Gibson. ABC News. "EXCERPTS: Charlie Gibson Interviews Sarah Palin. Republican VP Candidate Speaks with ABC News' Charlie Gibson in Exclusive Interview. Sarah Palin on 'the Bush Doctrine.'" 11 September 2008: ABCNews.Go.com. Accessed 15 November 2008.

p. 84   *I'm all about … not support this* Katie Couric. "One-On-One With Sarah Palin: CBS Evening News Anchor Katie Couric Interviews Alaska's Governor On The Ailing Economy." 24 September 2008: CBSNews.com. Accessed 15 November 2008.

enormous interest David Bauder (Associated Press. "Vice Presidential Debate Ratings: Early Numbers 42% Higher Than First Presidential Debate." 3 October 2008: HuffingtonPost.com. Accessed 16 November 2008.

Biden the winner Mark Preston. "Analysis: Palin gets back on track, but Biden wins debate." 3 October 2008: CNN.com. Accessed 16 November 2008.

If BS were currency Kathleen Parker. "Palin Problem: She's out of her league." 26 September 2008: NationalReview.com. Accessed 1 December 2008.

p. 85   *a fatal cancer* Danny Shea. "David Brooks: Sarah Palin 'Represents A Fatal Cancer To The Republican Party'" 8 October 2008: HuffingtonPost.com. Accessed 1 December 2008.

What on earth Christopher Buckley. "Sorry, Dad, I'm Voting for Obama." 10 October 2008: TheDailyBeast.com. Letterman, for his part, was merciless. McCain's recent visit to New York to introduce Palin to world leaders at the United Nations, he said, was like "take-your-daughter-to-work day." David Bauder (Associated Press). "Letterman Attacks McCain Day 2: 'I Feel Like An Ugly Date'" 25 September 2008: HuffingtonPost.com. Accessed 16 November 2008.

palling around with terrorists CNN. "Fact Check: Is Obama 'palling around with terrorists'?" 5 October 2008: CNN.com. Accessed 16 November 2008.

p. 86   *Off with his head!* Evan Thomas. "Secrets of the 2008 Campaign: The Final Days: Obama was leading in the polls, even in red states like Virginia. But McCain almost seemed to glory in being the underdog." 6 November 2008: Newsweek.com. Accessed 16 November 2008.

hadn't heard them Michael Falcone. "Palin Calls Reported Attacks 'Atrocious and Unacceptable.' 20 October 2008: NYTimes.com.

that one ABC News. "Debate Verdict: John McCain, Barack Obama Exchange Blows, No Knockouts." 8 October 2008: ABCNews.go.com. Accessed 16 November 2008.

54 Obama 30 McCain Paul Steinhauser. "Obama picks up second debate win, poll says." 8 October 2008: CNN.com. Accessed 16 November 2008.

unlawfully abused her power Matt Apuzzo. "Troopergate Report: Palin 'Unlawfully Abused Her Authority.'" 10 October 2008: HuffingtonPost.com. Accessed 16 November 2008.

cleared of any legal wrongdoing Lisa Demer. "Palin says report vindicates her. Governor offers no apologies for her role in 'Tasergate.' 12 October 2008: ADN.com. Accessed 16 November 2008.

p. 87   *a decent family man* Secret service: Evan Thomas. "Secrets of the 2008 Campaign: The Great Debates: McCain bridled at reducing his opinions to sound bites. Obama prepped as if he were taking the bar exam—nothing was left to chance." 6 November 2008. Newsweek.com. Accessed 16 November 2008. Minnesota rally: Newsweek.com. Accessed 16 November 2008. Video of rally: TPM. "McCain: Be respectful, Obama is a decent man. *CROWD BOOS!*" 10 October 2008: YouTube.com. Accessed 16 November 2008.

McCain decided to avoid attacks Evan Thomas. "Secrets of the 2008 Campaign: The Great Debates: McCain bridled at reducing his opinions to sound bites. Obama prepped as if he were taking the bar exam—nothing was left to chance." 6 November 2008: Newsweek.com. Accessed 16 November 2008.

We need to know ... Justice Department Russell Goldman. "Barack Obama, John McCain Get Feisty in Final Presidential Debate Before Election Day." 16 October 2008: ABCNews.go.com. Accessed 16 November 2008.

campaigned in Toledo, Ohio Jake Tapper. "'Spread the Wealth'?" 14 October 2008: ABCNews.com. Accessed 25 November 2008.

Joe wants ... working Americans Commission on Presidential Debates. "The Third McCain-Obama Presidential Debate." 15 October 2008: Debates.org. Accessed 25 November 2008.

p. 88 *CNN's post-debate survey* Paul Steinhauser. "Poll: Debate watchers say Obama wins." October 2008: CNN.com. Accessed 16 November 2008.

Obama's plan Robert Barnes. "Joe the Plumber: Not a Licensed Plumber." 16 October 2008: WashingtonPost.com. Accessed 25 November 2008.

Is there ...this way Pam Spaulding. "Video and transcript of Powell's endorsement; Barack Obama's response." 19 October 2008: PamsHouseBlend.com. Accessed 25 November 2008. Photo: Platon. "Service." 29 September 2008: NewYorker.com.

p. 89 *We need ... transformational qualities* MSNBC. "Powell endorses Obama for president. Republican ex-secretary of state calls Democrat 'transformational figure.'" 19 October 2008: MSNBC.MSN.com. Accessed 16 November 2008. Transcript:

p. 90 *three million people* Greg Sargent. "Obama Raises Over $150 Million In September." 19 October 2008: TalkingPointsMemo.com. Accessed 16 November 2008. A later study found that because of repeat donations Obama received about the same fraction of contributions from individuals who gave less than $200 in total as George W. Bush and John Kerry: 24 percent compared to 25 percent and 20 percent respectively. McCain raised 21 percent of his funds from donors who gave less than $200. At the other end of spectrum, donors who gave $1,000 or more accounted for 47 percent of the funds raised by Obama, 60 percent of Bush's, 56 percent of Kerry's, and 59 percent of those raised by McCain. Michael Luo . "Study: Many Obama Small Donors Really Weren't." 24 November 2008: NYTimes.com.

margin of the campaign Mark Murray. "Poll: Obama opens biggest lead over McCain: Dem leads rival by 10 points among registered voters in NBC/WSJ survey." 23 October 2008: MSNBC.MSN.com. Accessed 16 November 2008.

clothes for her husband Jeanne Cummings. "RNC shells out $150K for Palin fashion." 22 October 2008: Politico.com. Accessed 16 November 2008.

pay for some items Newsweek. "Hackers and Spending Sprees." 5 November 2008. Newsweek.com. Accessed 5 December 2008.

extravagant to many "Wasilla Hillbillies looting Neiman Marcus from coast to coast" said one Republican staff person, in a comment that was widely reported. Sam Stein. "Palin Clothes Spending Has Dems Salivating, Republicans Disgusted. 22 October 2008: HuffingtonPost.com. Slideshow: HuffingtonPost.com. Accessed 16 November 2008. Subsequent reports showed the R.N.C. spent an additional $110,000 on hair and makeup consultants for Palin. Michael Luo. "McCain Campaign Spent $110,000 on Palin's Stylists." 4 December 2008: NYTimes.com. Accessed 5 December 2008.

p. 91 *For the first time ... positive one* Mark Murray. "Poll: Obama opens biggest lead over McCain: Dem leads rival by 10 points among registered voters in NBC/WSJ survey." 23 October 2008: MSNBC.MSN.com. Accessed 16 November 2008.

23 to 25 October Daniel Nasaw. "Obama pauses campaign to visit ailing grandmother." 21 October 2008: Guardian.co.uk. Madelyn Dunham died on 3 November. Shailagh Murray. "Obama's Grandmother Dies." 3 November 2008: WashingtonPost.com. Accessed 16 November 2008.

Sunrise, Florida Associated Press. "Bill Clinton heralds Obama as 'America's future' at Fla. Rally." 30 October 2008: CBC.ca. Accessed 25 November 2008.

watched the program David Bauder, Associated Press. "Barack Obama Infomercial Ratings: 33.6 Million Watch Across All Networks." 30 October 2008: HuffingtonPost.com. Accessed 16 November 2008. Video: Obama for America. "American Stories, American Solutions: 30 Minute Special." 29 October 2008: YouTube.com. Accessed 16 November 2008.

p. 92 *Kissimmee, Florida* Jim Stratton. "Barack Obama, Bill Clinton rally for crowd of 35,000 in Kissimmee." 30 October 2008: OrlandoSentinel.com. Accessed 25 November 2008.

distribution channels Satellite channel: Ben Smith. "The Obama Channel." 1 October 2008: Politico.com. Video games: Jake Tapper. "Obama Advertising Within a Video Game." 14 October 2008: ABCNews.com. Accessed 16 November 2008.

actually voted The Economist. "The ground campaign. Obama's earnest army: Barack Obama's get-out-the-vote machine is bigger, faster and smarter. 23 October 2008: The-Economist.com. Accessed 16 November 2008.

allowed to vote Leslie Wayne. "Party Lawyers Ready to Keep an Eye on the Polls." 27 October 2008: NYTimes.com. Accessed 1 December 2008.

p. 93 *same week in 2004* Associated Press. "Campaigns uncork get-out-the-vote operations. With just two days, most polls show Barack Obama ahead of John McCain." 2 November 2008: MSNBC.MSN.com. Accessed 16 November 2008.

107 for Biden Karen Travers and Rigel Anderson. "Election Night 2008." 4 November 2008: ABCNews.Go.com. Accessed 29 November 2008.

for his rival Karen Travers and Rigel Anderson. "Election Night 2008." 4 November 2008: ABCNews.Go.com. Accessed 29 November 2008. Obama ultimately raised $750 million in total. Michael Luo. "Obama Hauls in Record $750 Million for Campaign." 5 December 2008: NYTimes.com. Accessed 5 December 2008. McCain raised $370 million total. OpenSecrets.org. "Presidential Candidate John McCain (R): Summary" 24 November 2008: OpenSecrets.org. Accessed 9 December 2008.

250,000 by McCain Karen Travers and Rigel Anderson. "Election Night 2008." 4 November 2008: ABCNews.Go.com. Accessed 29 November 2008. Massachusetts residents contributed the most to Obama on a per-capita basis: $3.31 each. New York, Illinois and California were the next most generous: $2.62, $2.42 and $2.29 per capita respectively. Associated Press. "Obama fund-raiser shares proof of committee success" in "Ex-aide of Biden will fill his Senate seat." 25 November 2008: Boston.com. Accessed 25 November 2008.

still was substantial CNN. "Election Tracker." 4 November 2008: CNN.com. Accessed 16 November 2008.

McCain's campaign The Economist. "Signed, sealed, delivered." 6 November 2008: Economist.com. Accessed 16 November 2008.

outside the White House Elaine Quijano, Alina Cho and Jason Carroll, "Obama win sparks celebrations outside White House." 5 November 2008: CNN.com. Accessed 16 November 2008.

p. 96 *aged 65 and older* The Economist. "Signed, sealed, delivered." 6 November 2008: Economist.com. Accessed 16 November 2008. FiveThirtyEight.com. "Obama Outperforms Kerry Among Virtually All Demographics." 6 November 2008: FiveThirtyEight.com. Accessed 16 November 2008.

28.7 percent Martina Stewart. "Report: '08 turnout same as or only slightly higher than '04." 6 November 2008: CNN.com. Accessed 16 November 2008. A Georgia Senate runoff election on 3 December underlined the power of the Obama campaign. On 4 November, with Obama on the ballot, Democrat Jim Martin lost to Republican Saxby Chambliss 49.8 percent to 46.8 percent. Since neither candidate won a majority, a runoff election was scheduled. On 3 December without Obama to boost turnout, Chambliss won 57 percent to 43 percent. Chuck Todd, Mark Murray, Domenico Montanaro, and Carrie Dann. "First Thoughts: Obama's coattails." 3 December 2008: MSNBC.MSN.com. Accessed 3 December 2008.

Bush in 2004 NYTimes.com. "President Map: Voting Shifts." 20 November 2008: NYTImes.com. Accessed 20 November 2008.

control of both houses Nancy Gibbs. "How Obama Rewrote the Book." 5 November 2008: Time.com. Accessed 20 November 2008.

I wish … president. NYTimes.com. "Transcript: McCain's Concession Speech." 5 November 2008: NYTimes.com. Accessed 20 November 2008.

p. 100 *America … have made* CNN. "Transcript: 'This is your victory,' says Obama." 5 November 2008: CNN.com. Accessed 20 November 2008.

FURTHER READING

BarackObamaForBeginners.com is the best place to begin for additional information. The site contains an updated list of print and online resources, including links to numerous relevant video clips, a timeline, and a complete list of sources for this book with one-click access to relevant online materials.

The best biography of Obama is *Obama: From Promise to Power* by *Chicago Tribune* reporter David Mendell. The book, published in 2007, provides a comprehensive review of Obama's early history, and a wealth of detail about his political career from the Illinois Senate through his decision to run for President.

Obama has written two books. *Dreams from My Father: A Story of Race and Inheritance,* published in 1995 and reissued in 2004, is a memoir that describes his childhood in Indonesia and Hawaii, college years in Los Angeles and New York, work as a community organizer in Chicago, and trip to Kenya in 1988 to meet some of his relatives. The book offers numerous insights into the politician's history and the evolution of his thoughts on such issues as race, poverty, politics, religion, and his family.

The Audacity of Hope: Thoughts on Reclaiming the American Dream, his second book, written during his first year as U.S. Senator, was published in 2006. The volume has sections that are reminiscent of the intimacy that characterizes *Dreams* but is in general more formal. Obama describes his thoughts about the current political divisions in the country; tells the story of his campaign for the U.S. Senate; outlines his positions on such issues as the economy, health, energy policy, race, faith, and constitutional jurisprudence; and concludes, as in his first book, with observations about his family. Obama won the 2006 and 2008 Grammy Awards for Best Spoken Word Album for the audiobook editions of *Dreams from My Father* and *The Audacity of Hope* respectively.

The Rise of Barack Obama by former *Chicago Tribune* photographer Pete Souza documents Obama's career through early 2008 with dozens of beautifully shot black and white photographs.

The Internet is an excellent source of information about Obama. Websites that are particularly useful include the following. Direct links to all of these are available at BarackObamaForBeginners.com.

BarackObama.com. The candidate's website contains transcripts of all of his major recent speeches, videos of Obama, recent news, and basic biographical information. My.BarackObama.com allows first-person interaction with the online campaign tools described in this book.

Wikipedia @ Wikipedia.org/wiki/Barack_Obama. The online encyclo-pedia has detailed pages of comprehensively-sourced biographical information, and additional pages on key elements of this book, from Obama's father and mother to political events.

Chicago Tribune @ ChicagoTribune.com/news/politics/obama. The newspaper has an extensive biographical profile of Obama, an "Obama blog," an "Obama tracker" that shows his recent move-ments, a photographic tour of locations important to Obama's life in Chicago, and even a Quiz to test your knowledge about Obama.

Chicago Sun-Times @ SunTimes.com/news/politics/obama/index.html. The journal's "Barack Obama" center offers a constantly updated index of news related to Obama, access to its deep archive of stories about the politician, and photo galleries.

New York Times @ Politics.NYTimes.com/Election-Guide/2008/index.-html. The best single online reference for news reports, statistics, and interactive maps related to recent U.S. political history.

The New Yorker @ NewYorker.com. The magazine has published sev-eral informative profiles of Obama, his wife, and other key figures. Search for the pieces under "Obama."

ACKNOWLEDGMENTS

My first acknowledgment is to my wife Xuan. Every word in this book is supported by her love and encouragement. The good cheer of my son Marco buoyed my spirits. Macallan K. Nein kept me grounded.

Dr. Robert Neer, my father, and Ann Eldridge, my stepmother, provided spot-on editing advice. My brother, professor Richard Neer, helped clarify important details. My sister-in-law Erika Dudley, and nephew Teddy "T-Rex" Neer, offered encouragement.

A book is a team in print. Chip Fleischer is our leader: he brought concision and clarity. He has been my friend for 25 years, and I am proud now to add collaborator to the ties that bind us. Dawn Reshen-Doty conceived of this volume: it would not exist without her. The careful attentions of Merrilee Warholak and Helga Schmidt helped make this tome a reality; Christa Demment González and Doran Dal Pra helped make the world aware of it.

Since a picture is worth 1,000 words Joe Lee, our Illustrator, has contributed far more than I. The dramatic cover and careful typesetting are the work of David Janik.

Ester Murdukhayeva and Lydia DePillis, who helped research, edit and fact-check this book, were my back-stops. Ester studies legal and criminal history at Columbia College and plans to begin law school in 2009. Lydia is a history major who plans a career in journalism.

David Kravitz, who read portions of the manuscript, and Charley Blandy (my co-editors at BlueMassGroup.com), Steve Swartzman and Maureen Marzano deserve special thanks.

The last, not least, acknowledgment is to my mother, who continues to infuse my world with dreams and the discipline of aspiration. I hope this little book would please her.

ABOUT THE AUTHOR

Bob Neer is writing his dissertation to complete his J.D.-Ph.D. degree in U.S. History at Columbia University. He received a M. Phil. in U.S. History in 2007, and a J.D. and an M.A. in U.S. History in 1991, all from Columbia. He studied Southeast Asian politics as a Fulbright Scholar at the National University of Singapore and is a *magna cum laude* graduate of Harvard College. He is a co-founder and co-editor of BlueMassGroup.com, the most widely read political blog in New England. He lives in New York City with his wife, son and border collie dog. He is available for interviews and appearances: contact Christa Demment González at Steerforth Press at telephone 603-643-4787 or email christa@steerforth.com.

ABOUT THE ILLUSTRATOR

Joe is an illustrator, cartoonist, writer and clown. A graduate of Ringling Brothers, Barnum and Bailey's Clown College, he worked for many years as a circus clown. He is also the illustrator for many other For Beginners books including: Dada and Surrealism For Beginners, Postmodernism For Beginners, and Shakespeare For Beginners. Joe lives with his wife, Mary Bess, and their son Brandon, three cats, and two dogs (Jack and Max).

AFRICAN 8-1-934389-18-8

ANARCHI: 8-1-934389-32-4

ARABS & 8-1-934389-16-4

ASTRONO 8-1-934389-25-6

BARACK (.... 8-1-934389-38-6

BLACK HISTORY FOR BEGINNERS: ISBN 978-1-934389-19-5

THE BLACK HOLOCAUST FOR BEGINNERS: ISBN 978-1-934389-03-4

BLACK WOMEN FOR BEGINNERS: ISBN 978-1-934389-20-1

CHOMSKY FOR BEGINNERS: ISBN 978-1-934389-17-1

DADA & SURREALISM FOR BEGINNERS: ISBN 978-1-934389-00-3

DECONSTRUCTION FOR BEGINNERS: ISBN 978-1-934389-26-3

DEMOCRACY FOR BEGINNERS: ISBN 978-1-934389-36-2

DERRIDA FOR BEGINNERS: ISBN 978-1-934389-11-9

EASTERN PHILOSOPHY FOR BEGINNERS: ISBN 978-1-934389-07-2

EXISTENTIALISM FOR BEGINNERS: ISBN 978-1-934389-21-8

FOUCAULT FOR BEGINNERS: ISBN 978-1-934389-12-6

GLOBAL WARMING FOR BEGINNERS: ISBN 978-1-934389-27-0

HEIDEGGER FOR BEGINNERS: ISBN 978-1-934389-13-3

ISLAM FOR BEGINNERS: ISBN 978-1-934389-01-0

KIERKEGAARD FOR BEGINNERS: ISBN 978-1-934389-14-0

LINGUISTICS FOR BEGINNERS: ISBN 978-1-934389-28-7

MALCOLM X FOR BEGINNERS: ISBN 978-1-934389-04-1

NIETZSCHE FOR BEGINNERS: ISBN 978-1-934389-05-8

THE OLYMPICS FOR BEGINNERS: ISBN 978-1-934389-33-1

PHILOSOPHY FOR BEGINNERS: ISBN 978-1-934389-02-7

PLATO FOR BEGINNERS: ISBN 978-1-934389-08-9

POSTMODERNISM FOR BEGINNERS: ISBN 978-1-934389-09-6

SARTRE FOR BEGINNERS: ISBN 978-1-934389-15-7

SHAKESPEARE FOR BEGINNERS: ISBN 978-1-934389-29-4

STRUCTURALISM & POSTSTRUCTURALISM FOR BEGINNERS: ISBN 978-1-934389-10-2

ZEN FOR BEGINNERS: ISBN 978-1-934389-06-5

www.forbeginnersbooks.com